way to
serve

way to serve

Leading through serving and enabling

Eddie Gibbs

with meditations by **Brian Draper**

Inter-Varsity Press

INTER-VARSITY PRESS
38 De Montfort Street, Leicester LE1 7GP, England
Email: ivp@uccf.org.uk
Website: www.ivpbooks.com

First published 2003

British Library Cataloguing in Publication Data
A catalogue record for this book is available from the British Library.

ISBN 0-85111-797-X

Set in Rotis 9.5/13pt
Typeset in Great Britain by CRB Associates, Reepham, Norfolk
Printed in Great Britain by Creative Print and Design (Wales), Ebbw Vale

*Inter-Varsity Press is the publishing division of the Universities and Colleges
Christian Fellowship (formerly the Inter-Varsity Fellowship), a student
movement linking Christian Unions in universities and colleges throughout
Great Britain, and a member movement of the International Fellowship of
Evangelical Students. For more information about local and national activities
write to UCCF, 38 De Montfort Street, Leicester LE1 7GP, email us at
email@uccf.org.uk, or visit the UCCF website at www.uccf.org.uk.*

Dedication

It is especially appropriate that I dedicate *Way to Serve* to Andrew, my godson and friend, as he embarks on a life of service as a newly qualified medical doctor.

Acknowledgments

I would like to thank Stephanie Heald, Senior Commissioning Editor at InterVarsity Press, for her encouragement to continue this *Way To ...* series. *Way to Serve* comes on the heels of *Way to Go* and, hopefully, more titles will follow! Both volumes have been enriched by Brian Draper, whose meditations are able to say so much in so few words, which is the gift of the poet. I am also grateful to Jeff Simons for checking the references and rearranging the chapters in the final version. Thanks also to my wife Renee, who puts up with my long silences and occasional 'shushing' while I pound the computer keys and promise to shut the machine down so that we can spend some time together.

Contents

Introduction

This book began life as a collection of readings on leadership called *'Way To Lead'*. However, the further I ventured into the biblical account of the prominent characters I selected, the more I became concerned with servanthood. For our primary aim is to become faithful servants of the Lord. Others may bestow on us the title of 'leader', but 'servant' is our self-designation. When leadership becomes our overriding preoccupation we can be in danger of redirecting attention to ourselves. On the other hand the term servant does have some negative connotations that need to be dispelled. We may think of a servant as someone who is at the beck and call of everyone, and is expected to respond to their every whim. Service should never be servitude.

In the Bible we find a different picture emerging: 'servant' is not a demeaning term but one of honour, because we are first and foremost servants of the Lord. Our prior allegiance is to him, and it is in his name and under his guidance that we serve those around us. The 'servant passages' in Isaiah point forward to a Servant King as well as to God's faithful people being invested with that title. Supremely, we see the role of servanthood modelled by Jesus himself.

During the course of the next forty days we will be examining the lives of individuals who were called by God as servants among his people in a variety of roles: Abraham was God's servant in the patriarchal, extended family tradition; David was a servant, exercising his kingship in the context of a theocracy; Jesus' style of servanthood is the most challenging of all, when we consider his unique nature as the Son of God, and his willingness as the Lord of the universe to become a servant of all. We will also see how Jesus' disciples understanding of leadership was shaped by their own preconceptions, and had to be profoundly challenged, changed and recast in terms of servanthood for them to become useful as servants of the Lord.

In the church today, Christians serve our Lord in many different capacities. Some make their primary contribution within the church, and it is these individuals who usually receive the most affirmation, support and training. Most churches overlook the fact that for eighty percent of the congregation their primary calling is to build the kingdom of God in their workplace and network of relationships; or, more accurately, to be servants of God as he builds his kingdom.

In contrast to much that passes for leadership, servanthood is not a matter of control but of influence. We will see that although leadership may consist of our position in a hierarchy, servanthood is based on our various roles in a network of communities of believers. Some of us may be visionaries, others will bring skills to accomplish a particular task, while still others are team builders, whose very presence helps people to work harmoniously and with enthusiasm. Some servants are people who see situations clearly so that they can define reality, and can then act strategically. As we study the scriptures we will come to see more clearly the kind of servanthood we are currently exercising, even though we may not realize it!

As with *Way to Go*, the first book in this series, each of the following forty days provides a biblical passage on which to reflect. My comments on the passage are intended to stimulate personal meditation. Then, read the short poem, contributed by Brian, to help you to identify personally with the individual and the significant incident that has shaped or redirected that person in response to the Lord's challenge and leading. It is our prayer that as a result of your reflection on Scripture and self-examination before the Lord that you will not only be challenged but also changed.

Eddie Gibbs
Pasadena, California

way to
serve

part 1

Abraham

The father of all who believe

Don't just stand there!

Genesis 11:27 – 12:9

The LORD had said to Abram, 'Leave your country, your people
and your father's household and go to the land I will show you'
(12:1)

People who aren't going anywhere or doing anything in particular,
don't need a leader. A caretaker will do.

But Abram's family were a people on the move. They left their
comfortable home in Ur in Mesopotamia (literally 'the land between
the rivers', the Tigris and the Euphrates), and travelled along part of
the familiar route known as the 'Fertile Crescent', which provided
water, grazing and food for weary travellers along the way. The route
stretches through Syria, arching to the north of Canaan, and then
along the coast road of the Eastern Mediterranean to Egypt. The
journey was long and slow: they travelled at walking pace.

And yet having uprooted the family, instead of pressing on to
their intended destination, Canaan, Terah settled the family in Haran,
on the western border of Mesopotamia. It was not until Terah had
died and Abram was 75 that the Lord commanded him to move. So
for Abram and Sarai, discovering God's will required patience, trust
and being prepared to move outside their comfort zones.

At some point during this time, the Lord spoke to Abram in a clear
but unspecified manner. Was it a voice he heard with his ear or in his
heart? From that point on there was no doubt in Abram's mind that
the Lord was guiding his steps, and had a plan for his life.

The promise the Lord made to Abram was staggering in its
comprehensiveness, yet vague on details. If Abram had insisted on
a step-by-step plan, he would never have embarked on his journey of
faith. At the outset he had to be prepared to abandon his security
in response to the Lord's command to *'Leave your country, your
people and your father's household and go to the land I will show
you.'* Abram responded in faith to a glimpse of the big picture, but
knew little of the steps to its realization. It is only when we let go that

we can let God take us to the next step. *'I will make you into a great nation and I will bless you; I will make your name great, and you will be a blessing ... and all peoples on earth will be blessed through you.'*

Think back to a time of disorientation or upheaval in your life. Can you now see God's hand at work?

At the outset the Lord made it clear that faith in him was not simply a private matter, but rather had profound and far-reaching consequences. This presents a challenge to so much of our contemporary spirituality and 'churchianity,' which is both culturally marginalized and in many cases socially irrelevant.

In spiritual leadership discussions, emphasis is often placed on *charisma* (giftedness) rather than character. But who we are is of more significance than what we do. We should not overlook the significance of God's promise to make Abram's *'name great'*, which has more to do with reputation and legacy than celebrity status. Within ancient societies, as in many cultures today in Africa and elsewhere, your name describes who you are. In the Old Testament, God was not revealed in philosophical concepts. Rather God became known through his actions and faithfulness to his promises. The 'name of the Lord' refers to the Lord as his people came to know him through the experiences of life.

God's promise to Abraham, though frustratingly lacking in specifics, presents a great vision. First, this childless couple would one day emerge as a great nation. That in itself would require a miracle. But spiritual leaders are people who are prepared to believe in miracles! Second, he was to be blessed by God not as a sign of favouritism, but that he might in turn become a channel of blessing to others. Blessings do not come in ponds and cisterns, but in fountains and rivers. They are meant to benefit others. Spiritual leadership represents an overflow of spiritual life, which is spontaneous and irrepressible, making a difference in a multiplicity of ways. The blessing is left unspecified because it is open-ended, fulfilling God's agenda, not our own.

So Abram and Sarai set out with their family members and household on the significant stage of their journey – a walk-through inspection of the land the Lord had promised. They found that it was already occupied – in fact heavily populated: *'At that time the Canaanites were in the land.'* It is ironic that the land continued to be named after these original occupants long after Israel took possession, being called 'Canaan' (after the Canaanites) and 'Palestine' (land of the Philistines). The same holds true for the world that both belongs to the Lord but is disputed territory until Jesus returns.

In response to his journey of faith the Lord continued to appear to Abram. God was replacing his servant's belief in many gods by personal encounters with the one true God. Having seen something of the land and its inhabitants, the Lord reassured him that he had heard right, *'To your offspring I will give this land.'* That statement, as we will see in tomorrow's meditation, would both reassure Abram and Sarai as well as drive them to despair in subsequent years. Faith is often forged in the fires of frustration and affliction.

In two strategic locations, Shechem and Bethel, Abram built an altar to sacrifice to his God. Although he worshiped at the sacred sites of the Canaanites, he did not use their altars. He was determined not to pollute his worship of the Lord with their immoral religious rites. The servant of God is someone who acknowledges the presence of God within a secular and pluralist society. Wherever the Lord has located his followers they are first and foremost placed as worshipers. They have a prior allegiance, are obedient to a heavenly call, and are inspired and driven on by a promise of God.

'Don't just stand there!' For some of us this may mean a journey to places where we have never been before. For most of us it will mean standing up and standing firm to make a difference where we are. God's blessing is not to be sought on the other side of the fence, where the grass always looks greener, but where the Lord has already strategically located us. It is here, and nowhere else, that the Lord promised to bless us and to bless many others through our presence and influence. Wherever we are, that will require more than one miracle along the way.

The Plan

So, what's the plan? It seems like ages
Since we dreamed dreams of setting out,
Packed our bags and embarked on the
Journey of a lifetime.

I set out to find you, and in the process,
I hoped to find myself
Caught in the thrall
of your great adventure.

Since then, this pilgrim's progress
Has been slow. I know you're my guide,
But sometimes I can't seem to see the
Wood for the trees.

Where's it to end,
This endless waiting?
Patience is a virtue, I know,
But God knows, I have to seize the day.

Am I waiting for you,
or are you waiting for me?
I'd love to hear your voice,
Get a text or an e-mail which says

Go! But perhaps this restless spirit
Isn't just me talking to myself after all.
After all, looking back
I have felt your hand in mine,

and your spirit tugging gently,
restlessly, at the right time –
whispering softly,
'So, what's the plan?'

I think it's time to go.

How do we respond in crisis situations?

Genesis 12:10-20; 13:1-4

Now there was a famine in the land (12:10)

Thank God that the Bible is honest about its heroes. We can all learn much from the weaknesses, inconsistencies and failures of God's servants. A true but tarnished image is more help than fabricated fame. We need the constant reminder that leaders are very vulnerable people, and the more they are in the public eye the greater the challenges and temptations. And yet the Bible refrains from moralizing. It simply reports events in an unadorned way, leaving the reader to draw their own conclusions.

The true mettle of leaders is revealed when they find themselves under pressure and especially when events spin out of control. In our culture of sudden and unpredictable change, of job insecurity, market swings and just-in-time planning, business leaders prepare themselves by thinking through their responses to possible scenarios ahead of time. What can we learn from Abram's response to crisis?

As Abram and his extended family were travelling through Canaan the land was hit with a severe famine. That is hard at any time, but especially in a stuff-and-starve society of subsistence farmers. A famine not only meant dwindling food supplies, but also no seed to sow for the following year's crops. Yet this was the very terrain that God had promised to Abram. None of us can afford to be complacent about our 'Promised Land'. Under normal conditions Canaan might be a land 'flowing with milk and honey', or, to be less poetic, a fertile land of fruit and vegetables. But it was always vulnerable. Mesopotamia and Egypt had guaranteed year round water supply from their famous rivers –

Leaders constantly need to ask themselves the question 'what if?'

the Tigris and Euphrates in Mesopotamia and the Nile in Egypt – but Canaan had no significant river. The Jordan hardly qualified as it was reduced to a trickle in the dry months and could not be used for irrigation. Canaan was dependent on seasonal rains, and if they failed farmers could neither sow nor cultivate their crops.

God's people are not immune from the circumstances impacting the society in which they live. They must be prepared to be as severely affected as everyone else. Furthermore, Abram, despite his great riches in livestock, silver and gold, could not buy his way out of his predicament. Like the apostle Paul, we have to learn both to live with scarcity as well as with plenty, proving the sustaining goodness of God in every circumstance (Phil. 4:11–13). But it is a tough lesson to learn. Even Abram failed the test.

Was Abram wise to go south to Egypt to wait out the famine? Egypt was the breadbasket of the ancient world, and so it seemed the obvious place to go to replenish food stocks. But the rational solution is not always the appropriate one. The Lord may have other plans in mind. The Genesis account passes no judgment, but Abram made the move without apparently seeking the will of God in the matter. Sometimes when a crisis strikes we act first and then pray later, or forget to pray at all, which can get us into a great deal of trouble. Be that as it may, we find Abram's party seeking refuge in Egypt.

One thing soon becomes clear – Abram under pressure has become very self-centred and vulnerable. Adversity tends to bring out the best and the worst in all of us. Before they crossed the border into Egypt, with increasing apprehension, Abram began scheming to safeguard himself. Furthermore, he was prepared to sacrifice his wife in order to achieve his ends, reminding us that in those days women were generally regarded as little more than the property of their husbands. He was concerned that some Egyptian would set lustful eyes on Sarai and kill him in order to add her to his harem. Abram, therefore concocted a story, based on a half-truth, that Sarai was to say she was Abram's sister to any man making advances towards her – so much better than an outright lie, or so he thought. In that way

Abram would be regarded as an asset rather than a rival. His fear turned into a self-fulfilling prophecy.

Leaders often have strong self-preservation instincts that they bring into play when under threat, sometimes even sacrificing those they love in the interests of a greater cause. Actions carry consequences, and, particularly when devious steps are taken, the unforeseen takes over. Not only was Sarai callously handed over to Pharaoh's harem, but also Pharaoh's household suffered as a consequence of Abram's scheming. The storyteller attributed this great plague directly to the hand of God. Sometimes the Lord has to take drastic measures to gain our attention.

Our unscrupulous actions, as people who still profess to love and serve God, not only hurt other people but also discredit our witness. Pharaoh emerged as the person of integrity demanding to know why Abram had been so deceptive. He promptly handed over Sarai to her husband Abram and banished the entire family from Egypt.

They found themselves back in Canaan, with no mention as to whether the famine conditions still prevailed or not. Abram returned to Bethel to build an altar once again to worship the Lord. We would hope that he had by now learned his lesson, but we are all prone to repeat instinctive responses regardless of the consequences.

Years later, Abram whose name God had now changed to Abraham, found himself in a similar predicament. On this occasion, he was in the south of Canaan, in the territory of King Abimelech of Gerar. Once again Abraham presented Sarai – now Sarah – as his sister, with the result that the king brought her into his palace. But God intervened promptly, warning Abimelech in a dream that if he touched Sarai he was a dead man. Once again the innocent were implicated. As a punishment Abimelech and his wife, as well as the other women of his household, were afflicted with barrenness, which was only lifted through the prayers of Abraham who left that place with a stain on his character.

All leaders are flawed. So the lesson of today's story is that God's servants should never be placed on a pedestal, and that we need to recognize our vulnerability. That is why service should be exercised in a context of mutual support, submission and accountability.

Yet, despite his failings, or perhaps through the experience of failure, Abraham remains the spiritual father of us all (Rom. 4:11, 16). The renowned servants of God, no matter how great, are neither sinless nor infallible.

We deceive ourselves if we think that living for God is plain sailing through calm waters. Storms will kick up. Famine conditions may prevail. Adverse conditions will arise to test the mettle of our servanthood. We will either crumble or emerge stronger and wiser. Furthermore, Abraham's experiences reassure us that failing a test of faith and character need not be final.

Carried away

I got carried away by your amazing love;
Then, by your amazing deeds.

I got carried away by the way you
risked using me – of all people – to help.

I got carried away by the works you performed through me,
and even, dare I say it, because of me.

I got carried away by speaking
the words you gave me to speak.

Then, by thinking I could
speak words for you.

I got carried away by the sound of my own voice
(and there's power in the name of the Lord).

I got carried away when others
liked the sound of my own voice, too.

I got carried away, swept along on a tide of popularity,
Washed out to sea, set adrift.

Please carry me away again,
but this time I won't get carried away with myself.

Deferential generosity

Genesis 13

Is not the whole land before you? Let's part company. If you go to the left, I'll go to the right; if you go to the right, I'll go to the left (13:9)

Abram returned from Egypt having accumulated even greater wealth. But material prosperity does not necessarily lead to a peaceful life. It is more likely to add to our problems. Furthermore, at the same time that we accumulate possessions we can become spiritually impoverished. So Abram returned to Canaan a chastened man, needing to retrace his steps to the location between Bethel and Ai to rededicate his life to God.

For every faithful servant of God, life and worship must be closely integrated. We call on the name of the Lord for wisdom in handling the decisions of daily life, not only in times of desperation. The pressing issue that Abram had to address was the arguments that had arisen between his own herdsman and those of his young nephew Lot, caused by the fact that both **Wherever you 'pitch your tent' you must build your altar (4, 18).** the water supply and pasture were inadequate to support their livestock. Abram's leadership qualities are demonstrated by the way he resolved the issue, and in the attitude he displayed.

Leaders realize the importance of finding amicable win-win solutions to problems, instead of permitting them to fester (8). Should Abram and Lot fall out among themselves, they would become vulnerable to the alien tribes around them. They needed to remain united in order to stand; if they became divided, they would fall prey to their enemies. In any community, tensions are bound to arise from time to time. The causes have to be identified and addressed. Sometimes the solution may prove costly and challenge the faith of the leadership.

In some cases a solution will be to create space because we have become too big and too close. There's a right time to move out. The questions then arise: Who is going to go where? Who has the first choice? That is when the senior leader is tempted to pull rank! In a culture where age denotes seniority, and where the patriarch of the extended family has the last word, Abram breaks with tradition by giving Lot the first choice. Godly leadership is both gracious and generous in dealing with others.

Lot was given the freedom to choose, but discovered that he had to live with the consequences of his decision. At first-glance his choice was an attractive one. *'Lot looked up and saw that the whole plain of the Jordan was well watered, like the garden of the LORD, like the land of Egypt, toward Zoar'* (10). But covetous eyes are selective in what they see. Lot discounted the presence of Sodom and Gomorrah, refusing to allow their evil reputation to sway his decision. Apparently, he thought he could live near them without becoming engulfed by them – a big mistake.

Abram, in sharp contrast to his nephew Lot, looked with the eyes of faith. He looked *up*, and not just *around*; and he looked to the future in hope. Leadership is built on a clear vision. When the Lord opens our eyes, we see much more then those who are simply self-serving (14). We see not only for ourselves, but for others and for future generations. Leadership achieves significance when it leaves a legacy. But visions are not confined to the eye of faith; they need to be possessed. So the Lord commands Abram, *'Go, walk through the length and breadth of the land, for I am giving it to you'* (17).

Lord, help me to be generous toward others and trusting and grateful toward you, recognizing that grace is a combination of gratitude and generosity.

After you
You came after me,
and that's what I can't
always work out.
You came after me,
left everything you had and
came after

Me.

I was lost,
grazing in bandit country.
A sheep, to be
fed to the wolves,
and like a very good Shepherd
you came after

Me.

You became like
nothing on my behalf;
but in the process
you turned me into
something – someone,
because you came after

Me.

And while I still
get caught up with myself,
the thought that You
first came after me
makes me want, forever more,
to come after

You.

Who has the last laugh?

Genesis 17:15 – 18:15

Abraham fell facedown; he laughed ... (17:17)
Sarah laughed to herself as she thought (18:12)

We live in a culture that expects and demands immediate results with people always looking for a 'quick fix'. But the Lord does not operate according to our hurried timetable. He takes his own time, which can be extremely frustrating. But the months, and in the case of Abram and Sarai years, of waiting were not *lost* time but *learning* time. Faith needs to be tested to safeguard us from turning it into presumption, complacency, or even arrogance.

God had given his solemn promise to Abram, who was 75 years old at the time, that he would become the father of a great nation and that he would be given the land of Canaan. After Abram's devastating failure in Egypt, followed by his separation from his nephew Lot, the Lord repeated his solemn promise. *'Lift up your eyes from where you are and look north and south, east and west. All the land that you see I will give to you and your offspring forever. I will make your offspring like the dust of the earth, so that if anyone could count the dust, then your offspring could be counted'* (13:14–16).

But the years passed and fear began to gnaw at Abram's faith. He worried that his only heir would be his servant Eliezer – so he shared with the Lord what he was thinking. The Lord then brought Abram out of his tent and commanded him to look up to the heaven to count the stars. Under a clear desert sky an overwhelming number – more than six thousand – would be visible. So from then on, whenever Abram looked down at the dust or up at the stars he would be reminded of God's promise.

Twenty years passed slowly by, and still nothing. Sarai's biological clock had long since stopped ticking. Resentment began to build up and a growing sense of hopelessness. She complained to Abram that the Lord had kept her from having children and invited her husband to sleep with her servant Hagar in order to produce their long-awaited offspring. He agreed.

But when she became pregnant, Hagar despised her mistress and treated her with contempt. Sarai blamed Abram but he refused to intervene. She then treated her pregnant servant so harshly that she ran away. Once again the Lord intervened, first to reassure Hagar that she too would be blessed with more descendants than she would be able to count, and second, to renew his covenant with Abram and Sarai, changing their names to Abraham (meaning 'father of many'), and Sarah (meaning 'princess').

Abraham had heard it all before, and his faith had given way to cynicism. This is a distressing characteristic of servants who have become jaded and dispirited. It can happen to any of us. Abraham fell flat on his face and laughed to himself in disbelief. His store of faith was by now exhausted. He had come to the end of the road. But our lowest point can also become the turning point. At long last, the Lord gave a definite time for the long-promised birth of a son. The child God promised he named Isaac ('he laughs'), anticipating the joy that he would bring. Abraham had to realize that the last laugh belonged to the Lord.

> Reflect on a time when you have taken things into your own hands rather than wait and trust God. What were the consequences?

But Sarah also needed to be convinced. When three visitors arrived unexpectedly, Abram welcomed them with traditional eastern hospitality and invited them to rest during the heat of the day and to share a meal with them. Yet these three were no ordinary men. It became evident that two were angels and the third was the Lord come in human form. Such appearances ('theophanies') occurred from time to time in Old Testament stories (see Heb. 13:2).

This time, for Sarah's benefit as well as her husband's, the specific promise was repeated, that the Lord would return about the same time the following year enabling Sarah to conceive. Sarah responded just as her husband had done, laughing silently to herself at such an unlikely, indeed impossible, prospect. But no matter how silent the laughter, the Lord heard what was going on in her heart.

Sometimes God puts his servants in situations that seem impossible to resolve, while at the same time assuring us that he will work through us. Like Abraham and Sarah, we have to learn that it is not through our own efforts that solutions can always be found. On occasion we have to come to the end of ourselves before God begins to reveal his purpose in any detail. It is when the situation becomes laughable, that we face the rhetorical question, *'Is anything too hard for the LORD?'* (18:14). When Isaac was born, right on time and the proud parents named him 'Isaac' as they were instructed to do, then they came to appreciate that it is God who always has the last laugh.

In just a few paragraphs we have summarized twenty-five years of anguish, bordering at times on despair. It is only with hindsight that we come to rejoice at the faithfulness of God. In recounting our own experiences we must refrain from dwelling exclusively on the triumphs, by confessing our doubts and disappointments along the way. Only by being frank can we be helpful, rather than set up ideals that are not only unrealistic but also dishonest. This is a valuable contribution that older Christians can make in mentoring younger Christians if they are prepared to be honest in recounting their experiences. Some lessons cannot be hurried. Many years must pass before the laughter of unbelief gives way to chuckles of quiet reflection.

It is only with hindsight that we come to rejoice at the faithfulness of God.

The last laugh
You must be joking.
Here I am at my wit's end
and you tell me to reach for the stars?

I had high hopes
that we were going to
change the world together,

Give birth to a dream,
leave a plentiful inheritance,
create a future together.

You're having me on,
and it might be funny
if it wasn't true.

Have faith, you say?
It's easier said than done
when you've fallen on barren times.

So, an heir looms, you say?
Get ready? Well, I'm waiting,
And wondering just who will get to enjoy

the last laugh.

day 5 | The burden of knowledge

Genesis 18:16-33

Shall I hide from Abraham what I am about to do? (17)

It is painful to watch a person we care about make an unwise decision. Perhaps we ourselves have embarked on a course of action that seemed attractive at the time only to prove disastrous later. Someone older and wiser than us tried to advise us to act differently, but we thought that we knew best and now we have to live with the consequences.

Abraham and his nephew Lot had found it difficult to coexist because their herdsmen were constantly squabbling, so they decided that it would be better for them to separate. Lot chose the idyllic, well-watered, fertile plain in the region of Zoar. But one must not be blinded by first impressions, or fail to take into account all factors – Lot sets up his encampment near to Sodom among the cities of the plain. These were Canaanite cities with a reputation for wickedness. Sodom acted like a magnet, and before long Lot and his family moved into the city itself. Meanwhile, Abraham continued to live close by and was no doubt aware of Lot's vulnerability.

It seems that there was a second reason for the visit of the three men: they had come to destroy Sodom as punishment for its unbridled wickedness. Abraham accompanied his visitors for part of the way as a common courtesy. It is at this point in the story that the Lord decided to take Abraham into his confidence. Becoming a servant of God may entail learning things that other people might not be aware of, and such knowledge can prove burdensome. Privileged knowledge is communicated to us not that we might have power over other people but that we might exercise our responsibility towards them.

We are reminded that the Lord Jesus also took his twelve disciples into his confidence by repeatedly warning them of what would happen to him in Jerusalem. In the Upper Room, on the night before his crucifixion, he told them, *'I no longer call you servants, because a servant does not know his master's business. Instead, I have called you friends, for everything that I learned from my Father I have made known to you'* (John 15:15).

The drama of the Genesis incident is heightened by the author recording the Lord's self-questioning, *'Shall I hide from Abraham what I am about to do?'* He decided rather to share his intentions, taking Abraham into his confidence as a chosen servant who needed to learn the responsibility of leadership, especially about the need for righteous living in a wicked world. Abraham had failed to caution Lot, and needed to understand the peril that Lot and his family now faced. Leaders must shoulder their moral responsibility in caring for those placed within their charge. Actions carry consequences. They must care enough to confront when the occasion demands.

What else are servants to do with the knowledge they have? The most frequent response is to worry over it, so that it becomes an increasing burden, until it threatens to crush them. The Lord revealed his plans to Abraham so that not only might he learn a personal lesson in leadership, but also that he might turn that knowledge into intercession. By worrying we take upon ourselves burdens we were never meant to bear. Intercession consists of sharing our burdens with the Lord, and in so doing discovering that he carries the major part of the load. Effective servanthood is the result of earnest intercession arising out of deep personal concern for those for whom we are responsible.

The servants of God have to come to terms with both the judgment, as well as the grace, of God. Those who persistently act in defiance of God's revealed will must one day face the consequences, whether in this life or the next. The role of the intercessor is to place himself or herself between God and his people to plead on their behalf. Abraham was aware that Lot and his family were living in the city that was about to be destroyed. He cried out on their behalf, pleading with the Lord, *'Will you sweep away the righteous with the wicked?'* (23). He made his case arguing that God is always just in his judgments. *'Will not the Judge of all the earth do right?'* (25).

Unlike many human leaders, God does not act on hearsay. Here the Lord and his accompanying angels visit the city of Sodom in person, to see its wickedness for themselves. Jesus likewise came into a sinful world, not just to observe, but to suffer its violent opposition. Jesus also made it clear to his followers that they were sent into the world, just as he was sent into the world, so they must expect to suffer on his behalf.

The story of Abraham's conversation with God may seem like haggling. In reality, Abraham was probing the heart of God, seeing how far he could go in his request that some individuals be spared. Notice the respectful tone of Abraham's pleading. At no point was he issuing a challenge to God, but rather, the closer he approached God the more he was aware of his own unworthiness in asking. He was conscious of the fact that he could go so far and no further. True intercessors know at what point to leave the outcome in the hands of God.

When did you come to realize that the privilege of leadership is not power but service.

Abraham had prayed that the Lord would spare the city, but the following day he saw the appalling destruction that engulfed not only Sodom but also Gomorrah. Had his intercession been in vain? God had destroyed the city because not even ten people could be found there who were righteous. But, the Lord of all the earth did in fact do right. Lot offered the two visitors hospitality whereas his daughters refused to take their warning seriously, being influenced by the scoffing of the local men to whom they were betrothed. Even Lot hesitated, until the Lord seized his hand, insisting that he flee with his wife and two daughters. They escaped just in time to avoid being overwhelmed by a seismic eruption. This in turn caused an underground explosion releasing sulphurous fumes that fuelled the flames from below, forever changing the nature of the environment. The fertile garden was transformed into a poisonous wasteland.

Lot's relentless stubbornness was evidenced by his refusal to follow the Lord's direction to leave the plain and head for the mountains. He insisted on staying in a small village, close by. He was not prepared to move far and his wife hung back. She hesitated for too long, and turning back to take a lingering look she was probably overwhelmed by the sulphurous fumes and then covered by the salt-laden atmosphere.

Intercessors do not always get everything they ask for, but the Lord answered Abraham's prayer in that the Lord was welcomed into Lot's home. The presence of the two visitors had incensed the people of the town, who had formed lynch mob intent on gang rape. Lot had taken the extraordinary step of offering his daughters to the people of the town in order to safeguard his visitors. It is a sad commentary on the low regard he had for them. Although the city was destroyed, Lot and his two daughters were spared. The results of our intercession may at times be meagre, but the result is just. This story reminds us that although leadership may seem a very public role, the major tasks of leadership go unseen and, of these tasks, intercession occupies a major place.

Heaven knows

Heaven knows, you're in the best place
to make a judgment. But would you listen
for a moment? Spare us, please,

The fate that we deserve, and
Spare a thought for those who seem to know no better.
Perhaps, even, for those who do.

You can see for yourself: it's tempting to stray from
the straight and narrow,
and squander your lot in life.

Who knows? You may even change your mind,
Hold off the inevitable, see it in your heart
To forgive the unforgivable.

It's your call. But you can see for yourself,
because you've been looking all along.
Heaven knows, thank God, what it's like to be only human.

day 6 | Giving back to God

Genesis 22:1-19

God tested Abraham by ordering him to take his only son Isaac
and offer him as a burnt offering

Today's account of Abraham taking his son Isaac to offer him as a
sacrifice was one that captured my imagination from a young age.

I could see Isaac setting out with his father Abraham to sacrifice a
burnt offering as they did quite often; whenever he was close to one of
their Canaanite neighbour's religious places. At first, Isaac felt no
apprehension but he was puzzled by the fact that there was no
sacrificial lamb. Abraham assured him that God would provide a lamb.

They arrived at the site, built the altar and arranged the wood for
the fire, but there was still no lamb in sight. Imagine Isaac's panic
when his father took hold of him, tied him up and laid him on the
altar. Each time I heard the story I felt a cold sweat break out as I
identified with Isaac and saw the knife raised above me in Abraham's
hand.

But like all good children's stories it ends on a dramatic and
happy note. At the last possible moment God called to Abraham to
put down the knife. Isaac's life was spared and there was the ram
caught in the thicket that took his place. It was only later that I began
to wonder why any father would be prepared to do such a terrible
thing to his only son!

From an adult perspective the story of Abraham being tested by
God to see if he was prepared to go to the lengths of sacrificing his
son seems both bizarre and repulsive. When we hear of child
sacrifices we think of Aztec rituals or sensationalized accounts of
Satanist cults.

In order to understand the significance of this story we have to
break through our cultural barriers to see things through Abraham's
eyes. Four thousand years ago child sacrifice to the pagan gods was
practised by the people of the land and it is strongly condemned in a
number of places in the Old Testament. And yet Abraham was unable

to reconcile the demand that the Lord made to sacrifice his only and much loved son with the nature of the God he had come to know since leaving Ur. This God was not capricious and cruel like the pagan gods.

We are told that God was testing Abraham's obedience, and we see him passing the test, believing that God had some other outcome in mind. The Epistle to the Hebrews suggests that Abraham believed that his son would be miraculously restored to life (Heb. 11:19).

All who are called to leadership have to face tests of obedience. We are all inclined to be possessive to the point of turning God's gifts into our private gods. The longer we have to wait, and the more precious the gift, the greater this temptation becomes. The greatest test is not in having patience to receive but in having the faith to give back to God what ultimately belongs to him.

I have known Christians who have clung on to their ministry at all cost, considering themselves indispensable, refusing help, failing to train others to follow in their steps, and holding on long after they should have handed their position over to those with more energy, and fresh insights. To give up their role would destroy them, because it is that which gives them their sense of identity rather than their relationship to the Lord they profess to serve.

There have been three or four occasions when I have had to give back to God the very tasks that have given me the most satisfaction. In fact, I regarded them as my calling from God. Each time I argued with God and handing each one over was a painful experience. But on every occasion when I handed the work back to the Lord, he opened up greater opportunities for service. I had to be prepared to release the one in order to be freed up to take the next challenge.

In some ways giving back to God was not the most difficult part. It was handing over to someone else and then watching him or her do the very job I would have liked to have continued doing. I observed them doing it in different ways from how I would have done it, and sometimes I had to concede that they were more creative and effective than I. This made me realize that the time had come to move on.

Notice in the story of Abraham the same sequence of events. Having been prepared to give back Isaac the Lord responds with this reassurance. *'I swear by myself, declares the LORD, that because you have done this and have not withheld your son, your only son, I will surely bless you and make your descendants as numerous as the stars in the sky and as the sand on the seashore'* (22:16–17). By being prepared to give back the only son he had, Abraham was promised countless offspring. May God grant us grace not to cling selfishly and possessively to any gift or opportunity that he has given to us, but to hold them loosely. God has the right to take back at any time anything that he has given to us, without any explanation. We must resist the temptation of turning our ministry into our idol.

In what ways might God be testing you at this time? How are you responding?

What lessons have we learned from his experiences that parallel our own life? Can we honestly say that we have learned to trust God more as we have claimed his promises and proven his faithfulness? Are we better able to handle the responsibilities of being a servant? And have we learned to be a worshiper of God and not simply a worker?

Making the sacrifice
Hold on!
This wasn't meant to happen.

Hold on!
I've grown too attached.

Hold on!
Do you know what this will cost me?

Hold on!
You're meant to be on my side.

Hold on!
Talk about sticking the knife in.

Hold on!
I've waited all my life for this.

Hold on.
Do you know what this feels like?

Hold on!
I can't let go.

Hold on!
Can I?

Hold on!
I'm in your hands.

way to
serve

part 2

Joseph

The slave who became a
governor

Overcoming our past

Genesis 37:1–17

Now Israel loved Joseph more than any of his other sons ... His brothers were jealous of him (3, 11)

Most lessons in life have to be learned the hard way. For Joseph the hard lesson was adversity. He had to survive rejection, unjust treatment, and years in jail, apparently forgotten even by God. His life is a classic case study of the puzzling providence of God gradually unfolding despite agonizing delays. Joseph's story provides encouragement to those of us who may feel that we are completely off-track and are getting nowhere in life.

Through years of character formation Joseph was being prepared for the significant leadership position he would one day occupy. Skills can be learned quickly, whereas our character is forged and shaped over the course of the years. And early years are formative.

Joseph was born the eleventh of Jacob's children but the first child of his favourite wife Rachel. There was jealousy between Rachel, who for many years was barren, and Leah, who felt unloved. The atmosphere was further strained by each of their maidservants, Bilhah and Zilpah, jostling for position – for both of them had become Israel's concubines. Such a relational tug-of-war would give a marriage and family counsellor years of work. However, Joseph demonstrates the possibility of overcoming the scars of a dysfunctional or abusive family background. But he also had to endure some hard lessons.

Joseph is introduced to us at the impressionable age of seventeen. He was troubled not only by the tensions between the four mothers in the family, but also those between half-brothers. His father Jacob should have been the stabilizing influence, but he had a long history of deception and manipulation. Deceivers are usually suspicious people because they are themselves fearful of being deceived.

Jacob made no secret of his partiality towards Joseph, the son of his old age through his beloved Rachel. The gift of the beautiful robe, a ceremonial garment, probably with long sleeves and of many colours, was not only ostentatious, it was also a status symbol. It seemed that Jacob deliberately intended it as a snub to his other sons. Every time Joseph wore it his half-brothers were provoked to jealousy. It was not an auspicious beginning for a future leader who had still to learn the lessons of being a servant!

But Jacob then placed his son in an impossible position when he required him to act as an informer, to spy on his brothers. Jacob was still the manipulator using Joseph for his own ends with complete disregard for the destructive impact of his actions on Joseph.

Joseph only made things worse by telling his family of his dreams. In their culture dreams were taken very seriously as predicting the future. Joseph's response to God's revelation stands in marked contrast to that of Mary the mother of Jesus. After the shepherds came to her with the news of the appearance of angels announcing to them that the Messiah had been born, they immediately rushed out to tell everybody. But in contrast, *'Mary treasured up all these things and pondered them in her heart'* (Luke 2:19). Some truths from God are given for us to reflect upon rather than for us to blurt out.

On hearing about the dreams, Jacob's response was to rebuke his son, but he knew that dreams could not be ignored. While running away from his brother Esau, whom he had cheated, he had dreamt of a ladder reaching up to heaven with angels ascending and descending upon it. With that dream he realized that God had not abandoned him and the Lord repeated the promise he had given to his grandfather Abraham of a large family that would become a blessing to all the families of the earth. On waking from his dream he had declared, *'Surely the LORD is in this place, and I was not aware of it! ... How awesome is this place! This is none other than the house of God; this is the gate of heaven'* (Gen. 28:16–17). How then could he now dismiss the dreams of his young son?

Joseph's family situation had reached an impossible state of affairs. By the time he reaches his brothers in Dothan, they were prepared to physically harm and even kill him. Without warning, a chapter in his life was about to come to an end.

Many of life's greatest challenges come out of the blue so that we have no time to anticipate them, still less prepare for them. What then can we learn from Joseph's traumatic situation? Often, as a young person, we do not have the wisdom to handle the knowledge that we have been given or acquired – wisdom comes with learning what to do with what we know. Second, we sometimes bring problems upon ourselves that could have been avoided if we had kept our own counsel. Third, in the making of a leader there is often a time of breaking – we need to learn the hard lesson of being prepared to die to self that we might live for God rather than allowing our ego to become inflated by what God has revealed to us.

What situation do you need wisdom for today?

Dream on

It's always been a dream of mine
to climb to the very top.

I dreamed in high-resolution
of sell-out shows, TV appearances,
of what tomorrow might bring.

I dreamed I'd turn the world itself
Upside down.

Dream on, you said,
As you turned my world
upside down instead.

My ways are not your ways.
The last shall be first,
and the first shall be last.

It's time to wake up. To open my eyes
to new things, to divine possibilities.
And turn from sleep to waking dreams.

A day-dream believer.

day 8 | Whatever our circumstances God is with us

Genesis 39:1–23

But the LORD was with Joseph, no matter where he found himself, and others came to realize that the LORD was with him.

Egypt was the place of no return. But God had plans for Joseph and we read repeatedly that *'the LORD was with him'*. During his years as a slave in the house of Potiphar, as a high ranking officer in the court of Pharaoh, and then as a prisoner who had been unjustly accused, we see the hand of God on his life (39:2, 21). In both situations Joseph had to learn important lessons to prepare him for his future position in Egypt, of which he had no idea. It is only with hindsight that we have 20/20 vision. A leader is someone who refuses to be defined and conditioned by outward circumstances.

A good leader is also someone who has first learned to serve well. Potiphar soon realized that Joseph was a person of integrity. Because he was capable, and prospered in all that he did, Potiphar was able to trust Joseph with increasing responsibilities, until he handed over all his household business affairs. A reputation is not built in a day, but through establishing a consistent track record of reliability. The Lord blessed Potiphar through Joseph, not only in recognition of his fair treatment, but also for the sake of Joseph, who needed every encouragement that the Lord was indeed with him.

Once again becoming a favourite placed Joseph in a precarious position. Being rewarded with rapid promotion stirs resentment in others who feel sidelined. On this occasion the threat came in the form of sexual advances by Potiphar's wife. She was not content simply to give him an invitation to sleep with her, but to pressure him relentlessly. The fact that he was extremely handsome and desirable fuelled her passion. Yielding to sexual temptation has been the downfall of many a leader, but Joseph remained firm, refusing to exploit his position and to betray the trust that had been placed upon him by Potiphar. He recognized that there were boundaries that he must not cross. He firmly refused her advances, even to the point of fleeing as she tore the robe from his back.

We would like to think that his integrity would be immediately rewarded. But God had longer-term aims in view.

Potiphar accepted the word of his wife against Joseph. On the testimony of his wife he had to act to vindicate her. Joseph was unable to provide convincing evidence to deny her vicious and false accusation. Leaders must be prepared to find themselves become the target of baseless charges and unfair comments. Centuries later, Jesus would reassure his followers, *'Blessed are those who are persecuted because of righteousness, for theirs is the kingdom of heaven'* (Matt. 5:10).

We are left wondering whether Potiphar was really convinced by his wife's conniving. If so, why did he not simply have Joseph executed rather than placing him in the prison of which he was the governor? However, we must not assume that Joseph was treated as a privileged prisoner. It is significant that he was placed in the prison tower, the high-security wing, where Pharaoh's prisoners were confined. Yet there in prison, we find Joseph once again demonstrating his trustworthiness and competence as a servant of God. Whether in a palatial villa or behind prison walls, Joseph discovered that the Lord was with him. He demonstrated his abilities by carrying the burdens borne by those individuals he worked alongside, proving himself to be a problem solver and work organizer. As in the case of Potiphar, so the chief jailer finds that life is more carefree with Joseph around to manage his affairs.

Joseph's hardships came one after another: betrayal by his brothers; sold into slavery; falsely accused; and then unjust imprisonment. Anyone of those experiences could have emotionally crippled him for life. The lesson we can learn is that our character will be shaped by our response to what happens to us. Hardships will either make us bitter, resentful and full of self-pity or the flames of adversity will forge strength and fortitude. We have to learn the painful lessons that many of life's advances are made in the midst of adversity rather than through favourable circumstances. We must determine not to be conditioned by circumstances, but rather rise above them – because God is with us no matter what happens.

Servant training entails learning to work without the need for constant supervision. We develop as servants as we learn to accept responsibility. Servants who are entrusted with leading organizations know that decisions will float upwards through the layers of management as a way by which people who report to them avoid taking responsibility. It is called 'passing the buck'. Good leaders work with people around them as they make decisions, while ensuring that they remain *their* decisions rather than that of the leader.

Is there an individual or a group that you can support through a decision-making process?

The response of both Potiphar and the chief jailer sound a warning not to abdicate responsibility when there is a capable person at our side. Delegation and empowerment always carry the weight of accountability. It is the responsibility of the leader to build in checks and balances both for the protection of the person carrying the day-to-day responsibility as well as for the person to whom they are responsible.

God is always with us
It's easy to see with hindsight
what we might have done differently.

Being wise after the event,
finding fault in the decisions of others.

Excusing our weaknesses
through the mistakes of the weakest.

But in the heat of the moment
it takes guts to stand up and stand out.

To take a stand for something higher,
To dream of brighter days and better ways.

Where is God when you need him?
Why have you forsaken me?

It's easy to see, with hindsight,
that he was there all along.

But it takes divine inspiration
To know that you can make all the difference

In the world when it feels that
he's left you on your own.

day 9 | Trusting God's timing

Genesis 40

But when all goes well with you, remember me and show me kindness ... (14)

In the few minutes it takes to read these twenty-two verses it is easy to overlook the time span they cover. The day-after-day dull routine of prison life would grind the strongest personality down. And in Joseph's day there was neither court of appeal nor scheduled parole hearings, so many individuals were left to languish. For some, waiting might prove to be the most severe of tests, especially when aggravated by adverse circumstances.

Leaders can sometimes be restless people. They are regularly looking for the next challenge, and dislike feeling confined or not being in control. But prolonged times of waiting are as important in character formation as in preparation for future service. We may need breaking as well as moulding for God to use us in the manner he intends.

Joseph was innocent, being punished on account of his moral integrity. He must have had to deal with the growing fear that the Lord had forgotten or abandoned him. And yet he did not succumb to bitterness or resentment. He became a trusted inmate, and was placed in charge of his fellow prisoners by the prison warden.

We are not told what offences Pharaoh's cupbearer and baker had committed nor do we know whether they acted independently of each other or had conspired together. But trivial offences could lead to severe punishment – and as high-ranking officials, among Pharaoh's most trusted servants, they were given special attention by the prison authorities.

The captain of the guard, presumably Potiphar, assigned Joseph to attend to the cupbearer and the baker. If Potiphar continued to place trust in Joseph, this suggests he doubted the charges against Joseph, yet he was not prepared to clear the record of his former slave. If this inference is correct, then Joseph's sense of injustice would have been all the more acute.

Those who themselves have suffered adversity are more likely to notice the feelings of others. Joseph demonstrated both sensitivity and concern in asking the chief cupbearer and the chief baker why there faces were so sad. The occasion now presented itself for Joseph to use his long-dormant gift of interpreting dreams in the service of other people.

Our service to the Lord will most often be in keeping with our gifts. Whatever our area of gifting, we must have the same attitude as Joseph in the exercise of our gifts – in utter dependence on God. He first acknowledges that *'interpretations belong to God'* (8).

Reflect on how you can remain utterly dependent on God as you grow more experienced in exercising your gifts.

Faithful ministry entails telling people what they *need* to hear, not necessarily what they *want* to hear. Joseph had good news for the cupbearer, but a devastating interpretation of the baker's dream. There are limitations in ministry. We may not be able to change outcomes for whatever they will face – only give people the forewarning to prepare themselves.

Both of Joseph's interpretations proved accurate. He appealed to the chief cupbearer to remember him. *'For I was forcibly carried off from the land of the Hebrews, and even here I have done nothing to deserve being put in a dungeon'* (15). Yet the cupbearer made no promises. Joseph had to accept the fact that the cupbearer was not prepared to risk taking any initiative on his behalf. Two long years were to pass before his release would come.

Our times are in God's hands and he is never late. That's a statement that's easy to make, but tough to live with when the going gets rough, and the days, months and years tick slowly by.

I can't wait ...
It's all very well when a thousand years can seem
Like a day to you, but

In a culture stuck on fast forward
there is precious little time to lose.

Time, in fact, is money,
So please don't waste mine.

Life is short, and there are
Things to do and people to see.

I hate to be a clock watcher,
But the devil makes work for idle hands

And I just find it so hard to
Slow down once I've got going.

I think they call it the
Protestant Work Ethic.

How long to sing this song, then?
I really can't wait to hear from you.

I really can't wait.

What fills our heart?

Genesis 41:37 – 52

Joseph named his firstborn Manasseh and said, 'It is because God has made me forget all my trouble and all my father's household' (51)

Joseph demonstrated his gift of faithful service in a variety of situations, as slave and prison inmate, in fact wherever he was placed. He didn't have the privilege of choosing either where he served, or the position he occupied. In each situation he worked his way up from the bottom rather than starting out with a privileged position. It is easy to think that if only we were in different circumstances we would be able to develop our leadership potential. We have to learn to grow where we are planted, recognizing that in impossible places, such as stony ground or in drought conditions, only God can make us flourish!

Some people go through life emotionally crippled, harbouring resentments because of being mistreated, unjustly overlooked or unfairly replaced. As we have seen, Joseph had every excuse to share such feelings. He was rejected by his half-brothers, sold into slavery, accused of rape, thrown into prison, and forgotten by the chief cupbearer. As we have seen, patience and trust in the Lord were lessons that both Abraham and Joseph had to learn. In Joseph we find someone who demonstrated resilience. No matter how grave the setback he seemed able to bounce back. Being a servant of the Lord entails being committed for the long haul. God's timing seldom conforms to our schedules, mainly because the Lord has a bigger plan in mind that is beyond our comprehension. Timing is everything.

We may be tempted to think that once we know how to use the particular gifts God has given to us, we are qualified for fruitful service. We may be able to acquire knowledge relatively quickly, but experience and wisdom takes time to develop. Wisdom means knowing what to do with what we know. It entails the ability to relate facts and circumstances but sees past the details to the big picture and the broader implications. Also, it requires humility to translate knowledge into wisdom, because a wise person knows his or her limitations.

Even as a young man Joseph was able to interpret his own dreams correctly. Then, later in life, he was given the interpretation of the dreams of two of his fellow prisoners. The prompt fulfilment of his interpretation of the dreams of the chief baker and the chief cupbearer perhaps rekindled his hope for the fulfilment of his teenage dreams relating to his own future.

Pharaoh had been troubled by dreams that his own wise men were unable to interpret. Then the chief cupbearer finally remembered Joseph. After two years, Joseph's dashed hopes were eventually realized when he found himself standing before Pharaoh freshly shaven and with clothes provided for the occasion. We might speculate that if Pharaoh's chief cupbearer had mentioned him earlier his request on Joseph's behalf would probably have been ignored. Now God's moment had come. Once again Joseph exercises his God-given gift in interpreting Pharaoh's dream. But notice that he did not claim the credit for himself; *'I cannot do it . . . but God will give Pharaoh the answer he desires'* (Gen. 41:16).

Joseph not only interpreted Pharaoh's dream, but also took the bold step of suggesting what practical steps Pharaoh might do to address the impending crisis. He outlined a strategic plan, and in so doing revealed an important characteristic of leadership, namely the ability to see the big picture with clarity. His strategy underlined the painful truth that the important issues frequently are not the most urgent. If the king of Egypt had responded with a 'stuff and starve' mentality the consequences would have been disastrous. Leadership is not reactive but proactive in its approach to an unfolding scenario. Joseph had not learned this overnight or through a formal study programme

When you are hurt, how can you see beyond your immediate circumstances to the bigger picture?

but through a lifetime of challenging and painful experiences. Pharaoh recognized leadership ability when he saw it: *'Can we find anyone like this man, one in whom is the spirit of God?'* (38).

During his prison years Joseph had overcome the temptation to become inwardly focused and small-minded. The fact that Joseph had learned to deal with his past, enabling him to forget all his troubles and his father's family, is evident in the name he gave to his eldest son: 'Manasseh', meaning 'cause to forget'. Also in naming his second son 'Ephraim', meaning 'twice fruitful', he recognized that God had made him fruitful in a land of suffering. This became the testimony of the early church, when, in a famous quote from Tertullian, a third-century leader of the church in North Africa, 'the blood of the martyrs became the seed of the church'. In many places around the world today we see churches growing in the midst of affliction and persecution.

The following chapters of Genesis record how Joseph was reconciled to his brothers and, at long last, met his father face to face. With the visit of his brothers in search of food to help them survive the famine conditions in Canaan, Joseph's dreams as a seventeen-year-old were eventually fulfilled. His brothers did indeed bow before him as the second most important person in the land, on whose decision their survival depended. As they bowed, Joseph remembered the dreams he had had many years ago. But he did not gloat. With the passing of the years, and the fact that Joseph, in accordance with Egyptian custom, was clean-shaven, the brothers failed to recognize their young brother.

Joseph decided to give them a rough time in order to reveal whether their attitude had changed, and as a ploy to ensure that they returned with his younger brother, Benjamin, whom he had never seen. His scheme revealed that the brothers had been living with a bad conscience ever since they had sold Joseph into slavery. Sin casts a long shadow. When they eventually returned to replenish their dwindling food supplies Joseph could not contain his emotion any longer, and broke down weeping in front of them. On revealing to them that he was in fact Joseph, they were overcome with fear. Now that Joseph had the upper hand how would he react? Would he exact vengeance?

Servants of God who find themselves in positions of influence and power must resist the temptation to use their position to get their own back. Joseph invited his brothers to come closer, to close the social gap and cross the chasm of fear. He told them not to be apprehensive or angry with themselves. Although they had sold him into slavery to be rid of him, God had been turning their evil intentions to the fulfilling of his own purposes. Joseph reassured his brothers that *'God sent me ahead of you to preserve for you a remnant on earth and to save your lives by a great deliverance'* (Gen. 45:7). This testimony was from someone who saw the big picture and had a heart set free from past hurts. In order to lead in a healthy, non-manipulative and non-abusive manner, God's servants need to deal with their own deeper issues, otherwise their judgment will be clouded and their actions may become destructive.

The life of Joseph is the story of an overcomer. The challenges and setbacks he faced proved to be the building blocks for his future ministry. Looking back, he came to see that, whereas during those long years of humiliation and adversity he had no idea how events would unfold. God's leading is usually inconspicuous and frequently along paths we would never have chosen for ourselves. Some experiences in life we would not have missed for the world even though we would not want to go through them again.

On the way
When you've got your foot down
and you're cooking on gas,
you can speed through the countryside
and the sun can be shining and
God's in his heaven and everything's
right with the world.

But who knows what's round the corner?
A red light, a breakdown, heaven forbid a crash?

Suddenly the place you were heading towards
seems like it's a world away.
You've got to make do with
where you are.

Put firmly in your place, if you like.
Even if you don't like it.
It can make you think:
if only I hadn't taken that wrong turn,
if only I hadn't taken that short cut.
It could all have been so different.

If only I'd have realized sooner
that my place is with you,
wherever we end up.
It's then that the journey starts to make sense.
And I realize I
wouldn't have missed it
for the world.

way to serve

part 3

Moses

The leader of a nation

Past failures cast long shadows

Exodus 3:1 – 4:17

Suppose I go to the Israelites and say to them, 'The God of your fathers has sent me to you,' and they ask me, 'What is his name?' Then what shall I tell them? (3:13)

Moses had enjoyed privilege and affluence in Pharaoh's court and had received a first class education and training for leadership. All that time his adoptive mother concealed the fact that he was an Israelite, the very people whom the Egyptians kept in slavery. Moses identified with the suffering of his people, but felt utterly helpless to intervene on their behalf. One day his frustration and anger boiled over when he saw an Egyptian overseer beating a Hebrew slave. In a moment's impetuosity, he killed the Egyptian when he thought there was nobody around to see. But somebody did see, and the Hebrew who was rescued reported what had happened to his people.

We all face the temptation to take matters into our own hands – but we may live to regret our impetuosity. In leadership timing is crucial and the intervention has to be appropriate. Leaders have to think strategically, bearing in mind the broader and long-term consequences rather than simply acting on the spur of the moment.

If Moses thought that his people would welcome his intervention, he soon learned differently. The following day, he intervened again to separate two quarrelling Israelites and then discovered that his actions were deeply resented. In a slave's world, beatings and killings were common occurrences. Life had become cheap, so Moses' violent intervention as a courtier of Pharaoh simply conformed to the stereotype. He was not a person that the Israelites were prepared to trust.

Moses' actions would simply unleash greater suffering upon them as their overlords retaliated, so they rejected his leadership: *'Who made you ruler and judge over us?'* (2:14). Leaders are not self-appointed, but rise to their position through the acclamation of the people. The Hebrews didn't even know Moses' true identity. Not only was he rejected by his own people but his life was threatened by Pharaoh. He had no choice but to flee the country. What a mess he had made of things!

Moses spent the next forty years in the wilderness of Sinai, living a solitary life, caring for the sheep of his relative, Jethro a priest of Midian. Perhaps he expected to spend the remainder of his life in that lonely and desolate place, on the far side of the wilderness, abandoned by God. He could easily have become embittered, morose and apathetic. With only sheep for company Moses had to learn to live with himself and to develop an inward journey.

Extended periods of solitude play a significant role in the preparation of many servants of God. Even in the case of Jesus, after his baptism, the Spirit led him into the wilderness of Judea where he was tempted by the devil. After enduring the test, he returned from the wilderness to minister *'in the power of the Spirit'* (Luke 4:14). There may be prolonged periods in our own lives when nothing significant seems to be happening. These years may not be wasted but a time for character formation.

God's presence with us may be unseen and indiscernible, for God is biding his time until all the pieces are in place and the opportune moment has arrived. God had neither forgotten Moses nor his people. As the years passed there was no respite in the sufferings of the Hebrews. They cried out to God, seemingly to no avail. But their pleas for help had not gone unheard, even though God brought neither relief nor deliverance. As someone has written, 'at such times we must resist the pressure to put an expiry date on our prayers!'

It was on the far side of the wilderness, in sight of Mount Sinai – as we might say, 'the back of beyond' – where God chose to meet with his servant. Later Moses would know God's awesome presence in smoke and fire on the summit of Mount Sinai, but on this occasion it was in an unremarkable burning bush in the valley below.

So often the significant holy places we encounter in life are not in sacred buildings that we visit but in unexpected situations that God appoints. Holy ground is a place of intimacy with God, yet it is also a place where we come to recognize the holy awesomeness of God – the former without the latter leads to a sentimental or presumptive over-familiarity.

Authentic holy ground is a place where we take off our shoes, and where we are invited to come so far but no further. Have you ever stood in such a place?

To the casual observer there was nothing particularly unusual in a bush catching fire under the fierce desert sun. The landscape was strewn with such bushes, so what was special about this one? The remarkable nature of the occurrence was only evident to the person who was really observant: *'that though the bush was on fire it did not burn up'* (2). The fire of God needs no kindling because it is self-sustaining.

It is significant that God did not speak until he observed that Moses had turned aside to observe the phenomenon more closely. It is to people who are alert, observant, discerning and curious that God makes himself known. All too often we have become too preoccupied and distracted, or plain apathetic, for God to gain our attention. Why should he bother to try?

As is so often the case the Lord calls by name, signifying that he knows us personally – our strengths, our weaknesses and our past histories. In the case of Moses this was particularly significant, because he had acted so disastrously by his unwise and inappropriate intervention on behalf of his people. His past failure had cast a long shadow. Only a life-changing encounter with God could release him from the crippling consequences of his past and set him on a new course with a profound sense of God's calling.

The Lord identified himself as the covenant-keeping God of his ancestors. Abraham, Isaac and Jacob all had their weaknesses and failures, yet God had continued to work through their lives. Therefore, there was hope for Moses – God who had proved trustworthy in the past would also prove faithful to his people in the future. Leaders must be unwavering in their conviction of God's faithfulness, otherwise they are likely to collapse in the face of adversity, under pressure from the complaints and demands of disgruntled people.

Yet, despite the dramatic nature of his encounter with God, Moses was still handicapped by his past, as was evident in his reluctant response to God's call. He felt that the task was beyond him. He feared that when he returned to his fellow Hebrews they would not believe him. He knew this from painful past experience. He would be returning to a people who had all but forgotten the God of their ancestors on account of the decades of suffering that they had endured. Their God had no name that carried any weight in their present predicament. So Moses pleaded to know God's name. What kind of a God was he to represent to the people? The Lord responded by saying, *'I AM WHO I AM'* (14) – in other words the one who is always there, always the same and who would act on their behalf in the future in fulfilment of his promises to Abraham, Isaac and Jacob. God is not two faced in his actions – he is always reliable.

We too must be assured, as much as Moses, of this foundational fact. As Moses left the wilderness and set out for Egypt to meet with the leaders of his people, he was still disturbed by his doubts. His lingering insecurity continued to show itself. But he obeyed anyway, and in so doing gradually came to appreciate God's hand upon his life. The Lord had assured him, *'I will be with you'* (12). In almost the same words Jesus assured his disciples when he gave them the Great Commission to go to all peoples to make disciples, *'And surely I am with you always, to the very end of the age'* (Matt. 28:20). This means that he is with you and me this very day and all our days and he becomes the basis from which our words and actions spring rather than being hampered by our past misdeeds.

I am

No one's interested.
I am.

No one's willing to help.
I am.

No one's going to give me a chance.
I am.

No one's up for coming to the back of beyond.
I am.

No one's bothered about who I am or where I came from.
I am.

What's the point? No one's listening.
I am.

Who are you?
I am.

day 12 | Make or break situations

Exodus 13:17 – 14:22

Do not be afraid. Stand firm and you will see the deliverance the Lord will bring you today (14:13)

In our service for God we are likely to experience defining moments. For some of us it may be in the form of a unique and unrepeatable incident that will leave a lasting impression on us, serving as a reference point for the rest of our lives.

Moses' experience in facing the barrier of the Red Sea after his triumphal march at the head of his people was one such occasion. What happened next is significant not only for Moses personally but for the history of his people. Throughout the Old Testament and on into the New there are repeated references to the Exodus and the parting of the Red Sea, allowing the people of Israel to cross in safety. This was the supreme act of God's deliverance, only to be surpassed one and a half millennia later by the death and resurrection of His Son for the sins of the world.

There are times in life when the Lord does not lead us by the most direct route but rather sends us on a detour that both takes us out of our way and prolongs the journey. In the case of Israel, God led them into the wilderness of Sinai, because he knew that they were at this time ill-prepared to face the challenges of occupying Canaan (13:18). After more than a generation of servitude they had the weapons but not yet the heart to fight against their oppressors.

The Israelites' change of route took the Egyptians by surprise, as they had expected the fleeing former slaves to take the coast road that led directly into Canaan, a distance of about 150 miles. Instead of travelling in a north-easterly direction they turned due south, which didn't make any sense. The Egyptians were led to believe that by this manoeuvre the Israelites would end up *'wandering around the land in confusion, hemmed in by the desert'* (14:3). They would then be at the mercy of the Egyptian charioteers who could move easily among them to mow them down.

With this fate threatening to overtake them, the Israelites experienced not only a supernatural deliverance but supernatural signs of God's continuing presence with them: the pillar of cloud to guide them by day and a pillar of fire by night (22). The Lord's presence went not only before them to guide but, when occasion demanded, moved behind them to provide their rearguard (14:19, 20).

When the fleeing Israelites spotted the cloud of dust behind them thrown up by the racing chariot wheels and the Egyptian army on the march, they were understandably alarmed. In crisis situations leaders face their toughest challenges – they are the nearest target for emotional outbursts and blame. *They said to Moses, "Was it because there were no graves in Egypt that you brought us to the desert to die? What have you done to us by bringing us out of Egypt? . . . It would have been better for us to serve the Egyptians than to die in the desert!"* (14:11, 12). Public opinion is very fickle, and leadership decisions must not be determined by the demands of the crowd.

Their situation seemed hopeless to human judgment – for they could neither move forward because of the expanse of water that stretched ahead of them, nor could they turn around with the Egyptian army cutting off their retreat. But Moses knew that it had been the Lord who had brought them to this place. God's guidance had been clear and should have been as equally convincing to the entire company because they could see the cloud of fire as clearly as he could. But perhaps they had not realized its significance. None of them could have known at that moment that the Egyptian army was pursuing them because the Lord had hardened Pharaoh's heart – to lead his army into a trap that would bring about their destruction. We are often left unaware of God's providential actions, until after the event – sometimes long after. There are times in life when God's footprints will be invisible (Ps. 77:19); it will seem that we have reached a dead-end.

At this point we see Moses' leadership stature revealed. His faith does not waver, *'Do not be afraid. Stand firm and you will see the deliverance the LORD will bring you today. The Egyptians you see today you will never see again. The LORD will fight for you; you need only to be still'* (14:13, 14). It was not until Moses lifted his rod over the sea at the command of the Lord that the waters parted, allowing God's people to move ahead into the wilderness and eventually into the Promised Land, while the pursuing Egyptian army was consumed as the waters overwhelmed them.

From this story we must not assume that the Lord will rescue us in every impasse. If we placed ourselves in an impossible situation through our own foolishness, denial or rebelliousness, we may well have to suffer the consequences. What we are considering here is a supreme test of faith, and the initiatives of God in leading us in unexpected directions in accordance with his own wisdom and larger purposes.

Has there been at least one experience in your own life that has caused you to look back in wonder, when God intervened in an unexpected, even miraculous way?

All at sea
Perhaps there's a pillar of fire raging ahead of us all;
it's just that we can't always see the light.
The only thing I seem to see is a black cloud following me,
and if that's God, then he moves in mysterious ways.

Eloi, Eloi, lama sabachthani?

I tried to take that step of faith;
we were singing a song about marching to victory
and it seemed to make sense: leave it behind,
and head for the promised land.

Eloi, Eloi, lama sabachthani?

Like Peter, I jumped over board, ready to rock
the boat for the Lord, make some kind of splash.
I didn't expect you to part the waves,
But you could at least have kept my head above water.

Eloi, Eloi, lama sabachthani?

As I began to sink I closed my eyes but could
feel your presence wrapped like water around me.
I was in deep, but when I hit the bottom you wrapped
me tighter still and whispered, 'I was here all along.'

Eloi, Eloi.

Where can I flee
from
your
presence?

day 13 | Shedding burdens too great to bear

Exodus 18:13–27

What is this you are doing for the people? Why do you alone sit as judge, while all these people stand round you from morning till evening? (14)

Many servants of God know the value of spending some extended time in the wilderness. Moses spent most of his life wandering in the wilderness of Sinai: forty years as a shepherd and then forty years as the God-appointed leader of his people. During the first period he had no idea that God would use that experience and his knowledge of the terrain as preparation for his life work, to bring Israel out of bondage in Egypt to the Promised Land of Canaan. If ensuring the safety of a flock of sheep had been a difficult task, it was nothing in comparison with the challenge of leading a disgruntled nation – for the euphoria of their deliverance evaporated just as soon as they had crossed the Red Sea, to be replaced by constant niggling that continued inter-mittently for the next forty years. Sometimes spiritual leadership seems like having to occupy the front desk of the complaints department on behalf of the Almighty! At the very least it helps us appreciate how God feels when we bring to him all our burdens.

Moses was a reluctant servant of his people. He felt the burden of his responsibility before God. Everyone came to him with his or her questions, unresolved issues and complaints. Consequently, he soon found himself carrying an intolerable burden. How many servants of Christ get themselves into a similar predicament because, like Moses, they haven't learned the secret of delegation? They too have failed to put in place an organizational structure and procedures so that issues can be dealt with at the appropriate level.

> Are you carrying burdens that really belong on someone else's shoulders?

Moses found himself with a line of people waiting for his attention, standing around from morning until night and many returning home without having even seen him. Moses could not survive this pressure for much longer unless he changed his leadership style. Fortunately, help came his way in the person of Jethro, the priest of Midian, Moses' father in law, for whom he had worked during his first sojourn in the wilderness. In addition to his priestly duties, Jethro demonstrated that he knew a thing or two about management! Observing Moses' weariness and the people's frustration, Jethro told him that what he was doing was not wise. By then Moses was prepared to listen to some sensible advice.

Servants need to remain teachable throughout life. In the midst of rapid cultural changes we must all be life-long learners. This is especially true for those in mid-life who may find themselves in a very different world to that in which they were trained to minister. The older we get the less teachable we become – we are too entrenched in our way of doing things. Furthermore, the task facing us may have grown beyond our level of competence, and so we have no choice but to learn new skills.

The majority of the cases brought to him were mundane and could be handled better by individuals on a personal level through daily contact. So Jethro's recommendation to Moses was that he should organize the people into groups of tens, fifties, hundreds and thousands. By creating this structure most of the issues would be dealt with at the appropriate level, leaving him free to concentrate on teaching the people, establishing policy and handling only the most difficult cases.

If such a structure was necessary to keep a nation together, how much more is it needed for the church to function as the body of Christ. The New Testament describes believers as 'members' – a limb or an organ – in the body.

The small group is the most appropriate place to discover and develop one's gifts in the context of mutual ministry. It is at this level that people find encouragement, feel that they belong, can be held accountable and find that their problems are addressed.

Whether a church numbers forty or four thousand, this basic cell structure is of prime importance. When personal issues are referred on to other levels it is often left too late by the time the church leadership becomes aware of the problems, whereas within the context of a small group that meets regularly, and in which mutual ministry is constantly taking place, people's needs can be identified and dealt with at the appropriate level in a timely manner. Eighty percent of pastoral issues can be dealt with usually in the small group context.

It is important that small groups do not attempt to deal with issues that are beyond their expertise. Serious problems need to be referred to those with the appropriate skills. There may be some individuals who are so disturbed, or have personal agendas, that will eventually divert, derail or destroy the group. Such a structure also provides a pathway for two-way communication. However, organizational pyramids readily degenerate into a hierarchy of control, especially in the present cultural context, with so many churches led by older leaders who have been schooled in an old-school management style.

The church is not the only organization that has found it necessary to flatten its organizational structure in order to facilitate a more rapid response to continually changing circumstances. Our cultural context has been described as one in which 'tomorrow arrives ahead of schedule'. People at the front end need to be trained and empowered to accept responsibility and take prompt action.

In small, homogeneous and static communities it is not necessary to develop a formal structure to ensure that individuals are nurtured in a supportive environment. The primary grouping of face-to-face relationships occurs naturally in the form of the extended family, friendship networks and within residential communities. However, when the community is fragmented, extensive and mobile, to ensure that everyone is accounted for, leaders have to intentionally organize the people for whom they are responsible. When he was a boy, even Jesus went missing in the crowd and his anxious parents had to return to Jerusalem in search of him (Luke 2:44). We can too readily assume that if we don't know where an individual is, then they are probably in someone else's care. When no relational structure is in place, then the community is a crowd of disconnected individuals. When community breaks down so does communication.

If Jethro were observing your life or mine at this present time, what would he notice and what counsel would he offer? Have we learned to avoid making ourselves indispensable? Are we prepared to delegate to others and to trust them to get on with the task? Are we only satisfied when other people tackle a job in the same way that we would? Furthermore, are we prepared to work as a member of a team rather than insisting on being a solo performer?

Missing

There I am,

walking down Oxford Street
one bright, May afternoon.
The sun has got his hat on
and everyone looks gorgeous
(apart from me, as usual).

There I am,

walking along,
minding my own business,
not exactly people-watching
but trying to spot a celebrity
(I once saw Nell McAndrew outside HMV).

There I am,

walking along,
and no one gives me a second look
except my reflection,
who glances secretly from Next and H&M and TopShop
(to check I'm still here).

There I am,

another face in the crowd,
one whole unit of spending power,
a credit card and mobile phone number
and sometimes one more bum at church
(Does my bum look big in this?).

There I am,

walking along,
minding my own business,
wondering what I'll have for dinner tonight
and who would miss me when I'm gone
(would I make an episode of *Crimewatch*?).

There I am,

walking along,
caught up in the fantasy
of my grainy photo on the news headlines –
recognition at last! – and a funeral at the church
(where at last they knew my name).

Empowering a team

Numbers 11:4–30

Then the LORD ... took of the Spirit that was on him and put the
Spirit on the seventy elders (25)

Despite the action Moses took in organizing the people into groups of
tens under a leadership hierarchy, the grumbling continued. Moses
for his part became distressed, not only because the people were so
discontented, but also because the Lord was angry with them. Moses
felt responsible as he shouldered the burden of leadership alone.
What more could he do to provide the leadership necessary? He
complained to God that their numbers were unmanageable as well as
their demands being unreasonable. He protested that he couldn't
become a nursemaid to each and everyone of them. They were like
babies who refused to eat what was put in front of them. Parents can
sympathize! Once again Moses had come to the end of his tether.

All servants experience a crisis from time to time, as their tasks
grow and new problems emerge. Like Moses we need to take our
concerns to God rather than simply internalize them or complain to
the people around us. On this occasion Moses was looking for spirit-
inspired intercessors to share the burden with him. It is significant
that the people never addressed God with their complaints, but
always laid them at the door of their God-appointed leader.

Sometimes servants in leadership positions bring the problem on
themselves because they consider themselves indispensable, or they
allow those who follow them to place them on a pedestal. But no
individual is irreplaceable. In each generation God raises up new
leaders, often from the most unlikely places. Too many leaders, for
whatever reason, are loners by nature, and the training they receive
reinforces that character trait. Theological colleges generally do not
prepare leaders to be team players. Rather they are educated for
ministry in a highly competitive and individualistic academic
environment. It is not surprising that this pattern of learning remains
with them throughout their ministry.

In yesterday's story Moses had to learn to delegate. In today's incident he had to learn to empower others. But it would be disastrous for him to empower the incompetent or those who would seek to operate in their own strength. A leader also must recognize that the empowering of others is not a ploy by which to abdicate responsibility.

The Lord instructed Moses to assemble seventy respected elders to meet with him in the Tent where the Lord was present among his people. There the elders would hear God speaking to them to assure them that what was about to happen was truly his will. Then he would take some of the Spirit he had given to Moses and distribute it among the seventy. This detail is significant, for servants in leadership positions must be prepared to hand over some of their gifting and authority to others.

Gifting is necessary if others are to share the responsibility of leadership. Authority is conveyed not just through appointment but through anointing. Spiritual authority is intrinsic – that is, it flows from within the person. The Spirit came upon the seventy as they stood outside of the Tent of Meeting in sight of the people. The cloud of the Lord's presence accompanied them, and they began to prophesy, indicating that they had indeed been inspired to speak on God's behalf. But this appears to be a once-for-all experience as there is no further mention of them prophesying – indeed the text explicitly states that they did not do so again.

Two of the seventy, Eldad and Medad, had remained in the camp for some unexplained reason. However, their absence from the meeting did not mean that they were denied the experience of receiving the Spirit; for the Spirit came also upon them as they were in the camp, and they too began to prophesy. A young man, who was possibly concerned that they might usurp Moses' authority, reported their activity. Joshua, realizing the potential danger in the situation, called upon Moses to stop them. But Moses replied that his interests could best be served not by limiting the prophetic voice, but by extending it. *'I wish that all the Lord's people were prophets and that the Lord would put his Spirit on them!'* (29). That would solve the problem of everyone thinking that they needed to come to him in order to consult God!

The experience of Eldad and Medad reminds us that the coming of the Spirit is not limited to human channels or to particular locations, but is entirely in God's hands. Several centuries later the prophet Joel took up this remote hope expressed by Moses. Joel foresaw the day when the Lord would pour out his spirit on everyone, so that sons and daughters would prophecy, old men would have God-inspired dreams and young men would see visions (Joel 2:28–29). His prophecy eventually began to be fulfilled on the day of Pentecost when the one-hundred-and-twenty believers in the upper room were empowered by the Holy Spirit to prophesy as an initial sign of the outpouring of the Spirit on all believers irrespective of age, gender or social standing (Acts 2:15–18).

The crowds who had gathered for the Feast of Pentecost were amazed to hear prophetic utterance after a silence of 350 years. This miracle did not occur in order for the international crowd to understand the message – all of them could speak Greek – but its relevance was to make them understand that the message from God was for the nations that they represented. Pentecost symbolized the beginning of the harvest season, providing a most appropriate occasion for the beginning of the spiritual harvest made possible by the outpouring of the Holy Spirit. Peter referred to the prophecy of Joel that looked back to Moses longing for the Spirit to be given to everyone. Today, we continue to live in the 'last days' inaugurated by Jesus, during which time he continues to speak through his people. His message is not restricted to the minister or leaders of the church.

Are you prepared for God to speak through anyone, irrespective of gender, social standing or age?

Are our established leaders prepared to relinquish authority to others? Do they believe that the Spirit who inspires and enables them in their service of Christ is equally available to others? This is not simply an act of delegation, for we cannot delegate functions to others that the Lord has already called and equipped them to perform. Both John the Baptizer and Jesus were filled with the Spirit, but only Jesus could bestow the Spirit on other people. As the Ascended Lord, he continues to bestow his Spirit to empower his servants throughout the church, on young and old, on male and female, and on people at either end of the social scale.

Power to the people
Power to the people?
But they like sheep have gone astray ...

Power to the people?
What are they going to *do* with it?

Power to the people?
Good Lord, what if they go wrong?

Power to the people?
Too many cooks, surely ...

Power to the people?
What's power, anyway?

Power to the people?
Whatever.

Power to the people?
Don't say I didn't warn you!

Power to the people?
I wash my hands of you, then.

day 15 | Stepping aside and handing over

Deuteronomy 31:1–8; 34:1–12

I am no longer able to lead you ... The Lᴏʀᴅ will deliver them to you ... for the Lᴏʀᴅ your God goes with you; he will never leave you nor forsake you (31:2–6)

The longer leaders occupy their leadership positions the more they are prone to consider themselves indispensable. They hang on to the reins after the horse has come to a halt from age and exhaustion. They have made no provision for a successor, thereby signalling that they want their period of tenure to represent the pinnacle of achievement. After their departure it is all downhill. However, the point of good leadership is not simply to leave a memory but a legacy. That comes about as a leader recognizes the right moment to stand aside, and ensure a smooth transition.

Moses, by modern standards, would represent a record-breaking term in office. He was 120 years old when he died shortly after handing over to his successor Joshua. Yet his eyesight was still clear and his strength remarkable for his years. So when Moses informed Israel that he was no longer able to lead them, he was not drawing attention to his declining faculties but to the fact that new challenges required fresh leadership.

We should consider our life span not so much in terms of years but in a series of chapters. Each transition point requires a time of reflection, consultation and prayer to know whether or not the beginning of a new chapter in our life represents continuity with the past, or whether God might be calling us to embark on a new venture.

It is never easy for a successor, no matter how gifted, to follow in the footsteps of an outstanding servant of God. Joshua could never be another Moses: Deuteronomy concludes by asserting that since Moses' time, no prophet has arisen to rival him; the Lord knew Moses *'face to face'* (34:10); he was called to a unique role at a most desperate time in the life of God's people. But Joshua would provide a different kind of leadership, one that was appropriate for a new set of circumstances.

There could be no doubt as to the identity of Israel's new leader. To leave either a leadership vacuum or a confused line of succession would have been disastrous for the nation. So Moses declared before all Israel that Joshua was his God-appointed successor, and laid his hands on him so as to impart the spirit of wisdom that he himself had demonstrated on so many occasions. Moses also used the occasion to make it clear to the nation that the Lord had commanded him to go so far and no further. Although he would not be crossing over the Jordan as the leader of his people, they had no cause for apprehension. The Lord himself would go ahead of them, and would also be with Joshua, who was of mature years at the time that he took over from Moses.

But Joshua had not simply been waiting in the wings for his moment to step on to the stage of national prominence. He had been a young man at the time of the Exodus when he had begun his service as an adjutant to Moses and was privileged to learn from Moses as he watched him facing situations and making decisions. Moses had mentored Joshua and gradually given him increased responsibility, as when he was made commander of a small militia formed to repel raiding Amalekites. He had also been among the reconnaissance party sent into Canaan to spy out the land and had sided with Caleb in presenting a minority report – that they should not be intimidated by the giant Nephilim but should march ahead to take the land.

When Moses went up Mount Sinai to be alone in the presence of God, he left Joshua to keep watch. The departure of Moses gave Joshua the opportunity to observe the idolatry of Israel as soon as their leader was absent. He came to appreciate how quickly and alarmingly things can go wrong, yet he failed to control the situation. Later, Joshua learned to wait in the presence of God when Moses assigned him to remain in the Tent of Meeting. Spiritual leaders must learn how to listen to God.

During these long years of service Joshua learned lessons of patience and meekness that would be essential to him when he eventually assumed the leadership position from Moses. Those called to become first class leaders must first learn to serve as first class followers. Individuals who are driven by ego and ambition become a menace to themselves as well as to those around them.

> It takes more grace than I can tell, to play the second fiddle well. Do you need more grace at this time?

When the time came for Joshua to succeed Moses, he received a double reassurance. The first was from the person he was succeeding, whom he knew so well. The second was from the Lord he was called to serve. The people also needed to see that Joshua was God's choice rather than that of Moses, otherwise he might later be accused of simply being the favourite of his predecessor.

Moses assured Joshua that the Lord would march ahead of them to gain the victory, and calls on him to be strong and courageous in leading his people against powerful adversaries. Just as the Lord had been with Moses throughout his life, in bad times as well as good, so he would be with Joshua: *'He will never leave you nor forsake you'* (31:6). So Joshua must not succumb to discouragement – leadership requires an unshakeable sense that the Lord will see them through to eventual victory.

Unlike many leaders whose later years bring embarrassment and failure, Moses finished well, despite the times when he faltered along the way. The people who had complained so relentlessly during his lifetime were succeeded by a new generation that finally acclaimed him. The leadership transition that God had orchestrated, and with which Moses cooperated, went without a hitch. He left a legacy that was carried throughout both the Old and New Testaments and continues to this day.

Joshua, for his part, was not only strengthened in his resolve by the repeated call of Moses to be strong and courageous, but also by the personal call of God after Moses' death. He was not destined to be a pale reflection of his former leader – God made it crystal clear that he would be with Joshua just as he had been with Moses. Three times the Lord called upon him to be *'strong and courageous'* (Josh. 1:6, 7, 9). Perhaps the reiteration hints at Joshua's reticence, for no matter how hard he tried he could not help but compare himself unfavourably with Moses. As he looked ahead he knew at first hand how daunting the task that faced him was. He had seen not only the fruitfulness of the land of Canaan, but also the strength of the Canaanites' walled cities and the prowess of their warriors. It had been many years since he had been in Caleb's party. Would they become grasshoppers under the feet of giants as the pessimists in their reconnaissance party had predicted (Num. 13:27–33)?

It is one thing to urge an advance when you are not the one to lead the charge. But now Joshua was the one who would shoulder the responsibilities of command. When calling for bold action, we all need the reminder – that it is easier to be bold when we are not the one exercising leadership. Only when we are assured that God continues to go before us, and that we are walking in his ways, do we dare to expose those who follow us to the perils of the journey, the battles along the way, and the risks in facing the unknown.

Taking off
Pity the poor flying instructor.

In the classroom, it's not so bad.
Lessons and scribbles on a blackboard

About how flaps work and how
wings gain lift through aerodynamics.

You can glance out of the window
and see the open skies, and know

that even if your student understands
how an aircraft flies,

it's you who will take off
and soar on eagle's wings.

But side by side in the cockpit,
theory fades into thin air.

The time comes when you must
look your passenger in the eye

and say, 'You have control.'
Handing over the joystick

Must take the steeliest nerve,
and the greatest trust.

The hardest time to let go must surely be
when everything's in your safe pair of hands

And it's suddenly up to someone else
to bring you safely back to down to earth,

without a bump.

way to serve

part 4

David

The shepherd king

day 16 | The heart of the servant

1 Samuel 16:1–23

We so often judge by appearances, whereas God sees a person from the inside out

It is crucial at any time for leadership to be of a high calibre, but never more so than when times are turbulent and when the leaders in power clearly are not up to the job or have even become difficult or deadly. When our story opens Saul, Israel's first king, had disqualified himself from leadership, having lost both the respect of the people as well as God's approval. But God is never caught off-guard. He already had in mind a servant to succeed Saul. The lessons are clear. First, servants must always hold themselves accountable to God and realize that they are appointed for the benefit of the people they lead and never to enhance their own power and prestige. Second, they must have an eye to the future, to see whom God is already raising up to work alongside and eventually replace them.

Samuel, a respected prophet in Israel, was disturbed by this political turn of events, particularly as he had been personally involved as the reluctant kingmaker. From the outset he had been deeply grieved about the motives of the people in demanding a king. He feared that the king, once appointed, would assume increasing authority and demand the extravagant trappings of power – consequently turning the people's hearts away from God.

Saul began well, in rustic modesty, but grew into an insecure and unpredictable tyrant. His life story stands as a warning now as then – servants are called to point to God, not to assume they are god! Furthermore, no servant can consider themselves to be irreplaceable. We must have an eye to recognize and make way for God's appointed successor – one that may not be our choice or one that we would immediately recognize.

When Samuel came to Jesse on his secret mission to anoint Saul's successor, he was nervous and the elders of Bethlehem were on edge. They wanted reassurance that Samuel's visit would not create trouble for them. Samuel's cover story was that he had simply come to sacrifice to the Lord, bringing a calf with him for that purpose. But they could not see the evidence of his real purpose hidden in his garments – a horn of oil for anointing.

Samuel knew that the Lord had already chosen one of Jesse's sons to be the future king. But which one? As would any Jewish father, Jesse presented them in order of age. The eldest son, Eliab, who seemed the obvious choice, impressed Samuel. But God intervened telling Samuel not to *'consider his appearance or his height for I have rejected him'* (7). In selecting any spiritual leader, physical appearance is not the primary consideration.

In Hebrew thinking the heart was not considered primarily as the centre of emotions as it is among modern Westerners. Rather the heart refers to our inner being, the deepest level of our personality, the centre of the intellect, which indicates something of the depth of their understanding into human nature. When we ask 'What makes so-and-so "tick"?' is the closest

Am I half-hearted because I have a divided heart?

we come to this ancient meaning. The motivation that lies behind a leader's reasoning and decisions should be the crucial basis of testing every true servant of God. Can they be trusted? Whose interests do they really have in mind?

The Bible has a great deal to say about the heart (Deut. 4:29; 30:10). We are to love the Lord our God with all our heart. The psalmist prays that the silent meditation of his heart will be acceptable in the sight of God, and not just his spoken words (Ps. 19:14). He prays for a broken and contrite heart and for a clean heart (Ps. 51:10, 17). In the New Testament, the Apostle Paul prays that the peace of God that transcends all understanding will guard the hearts and minds of the Christians in Philippi (Phil. 4:7). To the Ephesians he prays that Christ will dwell in their hearts by faith (Eph. 3:17). For every believer, and especially leaders, the core of our being must be centred on Christ and our lives filled with his Spirit.

But which of Jesse's sons fulfilled this essential qualification? One

by one they were eliminated, forcing Samuel to ask if they represented all the sons in Jesse's family. Their father admitted that he had
not included his youngest son David. David was sent for and brought
before Samuel. There remained no doubt that David was God's
chosen successor to Saul, for the Lord commands Samuel, *'Rise and
anoint him; he is the one'* (12). God's chosen person may be the very
one whom we least expect. Also, as we saw in the case of the youthful
Joseph, God often calls future servants who will be entrusted with
great responsibilities while they are young and impressionable so
that they can be trained in God's school.

Anointing oil was poured on a person as a symbol of God's
calling. The penetrating power of oil represents the Spirit of God
permeating the person and empowering them for their appointed
service. God always enables the person he calls, but that enabling
depends on continuing reliance upon the Lord for his strength and
wisdom. Humility characterizes every true servant of God.

The narrative then jumps ahead to the time when young David is
introduced into the court of Saul. His calling as a shepherd and
gifting as a musician were both significant in his new surroundings.
He was also introduced to the court as a warrior, which seems to
indicate that chronologically this stage in his life belongs after his
encounter with the Philistine military champion Goliath.

The court of Saul was a perilous place, with tension in the air due
to Saul's increasingly unpredictable nature as his jealousy deepened
into paranoia. As a shepherd, David had developed keen powers of
observation, for in that role he had to be watchful at all times,
keeping an eye on the sheep and looking out for predators and
rustlers. In court he used those powers of observation to watch the
daily dramas being played out from the vantage point of a young
minstrel who was ignored for the majority of the time. When violent
outbursts and dark moods possessed the king, it was David's task to
sooth him with his music in a manner that no words could
accomplish. While David's playing had a calming influence it could
not deliver lasting peace, only temporary relief. In a place where
individuals and cliques were constantly jockeying for attention and

influence, he saw hearts laid bare. He observed the ugly side of human nature. He also learned valuable lessons on how to survive in such an environment.

There may be times in life when we too face ugly scenes and difficult people who demean us by the way in which they abuse their position and wield their authority. In such situations we have to come to terms with the limitations of what we are able to accomplish. We must learn patience and gain wisdom to ensure that we do not replicate those same conditions when our turn comes to exercise leadership. One of the Psalms attributed to David concludes with this prayer:

> Search me, O God, and know my heart;
>   test me and know my anxious thoughts.
> See if there is any offensive way in me,
>   and lead me in the way everlasting.
>
> (Ps. 139:23)

Here speaks a mature servant who has not only seen a great deal of life, but who has also learned a lot about himself in the process.

Heart

They say the heart of the matter
is the matter of the human heart.

But Valentine's cards and Hollywood endings
have broken mine; they've

beaten it into a schmaltzy pulp
and sprinkled it with glitter.

Yet above the white noise
and the static, beyond the love songs

And the classifieds seeking
non-smokers with a GSOH,

an unfamiliar sound pulses; a voice
whispers 'Have a heart.'

And something deep down
seems to skip a beat,

and thrills at the prospect of
Giving myself completely

and being accepted for exactly
who I am.

Courage to confront

1 Samuel 17:1–58

Who is this uncircumcised Philistine that he should defy the armies of the living God? (26)

There are times in life when we find ourselves having to fight a decisive battle against a defiant foe. We can learn valuable lessons for such times from today's famous story. The armies of Israel were drawn up along Judah's borders with Philistia. The Philistines, who came from Crete, had superior weapons and were well organized, thus presenting a serious threat. This was a battle that Israel could not afford to lose.

The sides were unequally matched, not so much because of the relative strength of the armies, but because Israel by now had an inadequate leader, whereas the Philistines could present a champion to challenge and taunt the opposing army. In Old Testament times a battle was sometimes decided by each side presenting their champion, and whoever won signalled the victory of the side they represented, thus saving a lot of blood from being spilt.

At one time Saul might himself have fulfilled the role of champion. He had a height advantage over most of his people and had proved himself in battle with decisive victories over his enemies – even the Philistines. But yesterday's triumphs are no guarantee of victory today and Saul had become demoralized and vindictive. He no longer listened to God and was increasingly suspicious of those who served him. His dark moods had sapped his energy and under-mined his valour. So often in life the greatest challenges come when we are least prepared. Satan is strategic in both his timing as well as his tactics.

The appearance of Goliath was enough to melt the courage of the bravest. He was over nine feet tall, almost equalling the tallest person in the *Guinness Book of Records.* He was well protected by armour and leather coverings for his arms and legs and the cover provided by his shield. He was armed with a javelin, a spear and a sword.

Among the soldiers of Israel no one was prepared to confront him in combat. Any soldier who volunteered faced not just the peril and humiliation of personal defeat in full view of both armies, but the fate of Israel would be in his hands alone.

The boasting, bravado and taunts of one man succeeded in paralysing a whole army. The consequence was a standoff, which could not go on indefinitely. Time was running out, and the longer Saul procrastinated the greater the psychological advantage to the enemy. The failure of human leadership at this time serves as a reminder that oftentimes the people of God cannot match the world's criteria for strength. It is in our very weakness that we come to realize the strength of the God who is with us.

God's way of operating is so often topsy-turvy. His answer to the situation came not from the leaders at the top, i.e. Saul or his war cabinet, but from a despised servant from the grass roots. Didn't Jesus say that *'many who are first will be last, and the last first'* (Mark 10:31) in his kingdom? David is introduced into the narrative as a 'gofer', running back and forth tending his father's sheep at Bethlehem, bringing provision to three of his older brothers and presenting a gift of cheeses from the aged Jesse to his sons' company commander to ensure that they were well treated!

After forty days of facing one another, the battle was still no more than a twice daily shouting match. The battle cry of the Israelites represented little more than hot air. At least the boastful Goliath was prepared to put his life on the line as he cried, *'This day I defy the ranks of Israel!'* (10). But in the midst of this David had the spiritual discernment to see things differently. He recognized that Goliath defied the armies not of Saul but of *'the living God'* (26) who is the Lord of hosts (armies). The heart of the problem lay not in the height and strength of Goliath but in an army whose courage had melted away because they had lost confidence in God. But David heard the covenant promises of God to his people rather than the inner voice of defeatism or the defeatist chorus of those who surrounded him. His confidence rested in the voice of God in whom alone they could achieve victory.

David is indeed the most unlikely of candidates to be matched against the mighty Goliath. Despite David's youth and inexperience in military combat, he was presented to King Saul as the only candidate – that's how desperate this pathetic situation had become! But as limited as he was in physique, he was the one only one to see beyond the boasts of Goliath and deflate his challenge. He enquired of the men standing around him, *'Who is this uncircumcised Philistine that he should defy the armies of the living God'* (26). And that was precisely the point that Saul and his troops had forgotten.

When Eliab, David's oldest brother, realized that their youngest member of the family was prepared to do what they would not even contemplate, he and the other brothers became furious, and accused him of deceit and wickedness. Jealousy causes people to make irrational statements. Perhaps they thought David was simply displaying bravado in order to put himself in a good light, knowing full well that his offer would be dismissed out of hand on account of his youthfulness and inexperience. But David refused to be silenced, until eventually he was overheard and brought before King Saul. As he listened to him, Saul admired his spirit, his courage and his faith. Saul could still recognize leadership potential when he saw it. Perhaps he also took notice of the lad in order to shame his senior officers. Here at least was someone with the courage and resolve to want to defend the honour of the God he served. We know that David's boldness was not simply youthful idealism but arose from the anointing by Samuel that bestowed boldness, for from *'that day on the Spirit of the LORD came upon David with power'* (16:13).

David spoke with maturity beyond his years, reminding us that a servant who is dedicated to God may display a surprising spiritual authority. *'Let no one lose heart on account of this Philistine; your servant will go and fight him'* (32), he declared to the demoralized company. Then David informed Saul of his experiences as a shepherd in confronting wild animals while defending his flock from predators. In confronting a lion and a bear, David had learned the tactics of a hunter.

Saul was evidently impressed, telling David, *'Go, and the LORD be with you'* (37). Yet, I think, we must use our imaginations and read between the lines in what follows. Why did Saul dress the youth David in his armour? Was it to bring home to David the consequences of his decision? Was it to give him the opportunity of having second thoughts? The sight of him clumping about in armour too bulky and heavy for him to wear must have been a comic spectacle. But David was not deterred. He declined Saul's offer deciding to fight on his own terms, drawing on his past experience.

A wise servant of God makes sure that he or she does not attempt to fight against the enemies of God on the terms dictated by their adversary. David exchanges Saul's armour and weapons for his familiar slingshot and staff. Goliath was just a big bear with a sore head and a loud mouth. David had learned an important lesson as a shepherd alone on the hills – to fight on his own terms if he was to gain the advantage. It was foolish to mess with lions and bears at close quarters!

As Goliath saw the stripling David, he made the fatal mistake of underestimating his foe. He challenged the boy to come to him so that he could finish him off with one blow and feed his flesh to the birds. But the taunt did not deter David. He realized full well that he stood no chance if their struggle developed into a sword fight and a wrestling match. With the Philistine champion now well within range of his most effective weapon, David decided to act quickly and gain the element of surprise. Goliath had seen his staff but failed to notice the stones and his slingshot. Effective servants know how to use the resources to hand to their best advantage. The contest was over almost before it began. Goliath was struck between the eyes by a well-aimed stone and died instantly.

Has anyone ever tried to make you into somebody else? What can you learn from David's response to Saul?

David's single-handed victory had a dramatic effect on the morale on both armies. The Philistines fled with the Israelites in hot pursuit. But notice that David did not claim the victory for himself; instead he gave glory to God. He declared to the Philistine even before delivering the fatal blow, *'All those gathered here will know that it is not by sword or spear that the LORD saves; for the battle is the LORD's, and he will give all of you into our hands'* (47). That was a lesson David had learned earlier in his struggles with the bear and the lion – it was the Lord who delivered him on both occasions. As soon as a servant seeks to become the centre of attention, he or she ceases to be a servant.

Aiming high

The first shall be last and the last shall be first.

It's not an easy thing to get your head round,
especially when you're so used to finishing ahead of the rest.

When you're at the front of the queue, the top of the stack.
When you've spent your life climbing to the top of the ladder.

But what happens when you discover that all along,
having worked so hard and tirelessly,

having attained your goals and having fulfilled
the ambitions you set for yourself,

you discover that the ladder you've been climbing
has been leaning against the wrong wall, all along?

It's never too late. Amazing grace,
how sweet the sound for those with ears to hear!

It's when your own world is turned on its head
that you begin to realize the bewildering truth

That the first will be last, and the last will be first.

The destructive power of jealousy

1 Samuel 18:1-16

'Saul has slain his thousands, and David his tens of thousands.'
Saul was very angry; this refrain galled him (7, 8)

Of all the bad feelings that rise up within us, jealousy is among the most destructive. It not only poisons and consumes us; it spells danger to everyone around. A proverb reminds us, *'Anger is cruel and fury overwhelming, but who can stand before jealousy?'* (Prov. 27:4). The situation becomes even more perilous when the person who has authority over us becomes consumed with jealousy, as the young David discovered in his relationship with King Saul.

David's success and popularity quickly proved to be his undoing. For at the same time that the young David was in the ascendancy, King Saul was on the way down in terms of his power and prestige. Having begun well, and with the Spirit of God coming upon him with power, confirming his anointing for leadership, Saul subsequently usurped his power. The prophet Samuel, who was the one who anointed him now rebuked him, warning him that '... *now your kingdom will not endure; the LORD has sought out a man after his own heart and appointed him leader of his people, because you have not kept the LORD's command'* (13:14). Saul was now living under the Lord's displeasure (15:35), becoming increasingly morose on account of the influence of the evil spirit that invaded his life.

Initially, Saul looked upon David favourably, thinking that he was useful to him in bolstering his power. The young shepherd-boy's spectacular defeat of Goliath and the subsequent rout of the Philistine army had enhanced Saul's position. So the King decided to exploit his advantage by promoting David to high rank in his army and by sending him out on other military campaigns. Whatever the King demanded of him, David succeeded in his mission (5). So long as the credit came to Saul, everything went well.

But high achievers are likely to pose a threat to those around and above them. In David's case, the storm clouds began to gather when he returned home from killing the Philistines, accompanied by the refrain: *'Saul has slain his thousands and David his tens of thousands'* (7), not music in the ears of King Saul! These words became David's death warrant – the memory of that occasion lived on (21:11; 29:5). The valour of the servant had surpassed that of his master.

As Tom Houston points out, what may have also aroused Saul's jealousy was that Saul belonged to the tribe of Benjamin, famous for its skill with the sling (Judg. 20:15, 16), the very weapon with which David the shepherd-boy had defeated Goliath. That must have stung Saul almost with the force that the stone had struck the Philistine giant.

While David is playing his harp in order to sooth the king, Saul lashes out in a jealous rage, but David avoids the attack. So Saul's tactic turns now to get rid of David by assigning him to dangerous missions, hoping that his military boldness would eventually lead to his death in battle. In that way David would die a hero with full military honours, and Saul could

How have you had to deal with jealousy in your own life?

further strengthen his position. But Saul's strategy proved counter-productive. Not only was David victorious – *'In everything he did he had great success, because the LORD was with him'* (14) – he was even befriended by members of Saul's own family: his son Jonathan became David's closest friend, and his daughter Michal fell in love with him (20). Saul's jealousy boiled over into unrelenting hatred and fear – a toxic combination.

The lessons of this tragic story are clear. First, we must not allow jealousy in our own life, for it will eventually take over. Second, we must learn from David to be watchful and wise. It is a spine chilling moment when someone cautions us to 'mind your back'. We must resist the temptation to want to get even in response to spiteful treatment. Better to leave it in the hands of God to provide our protection and ensure our vindication.

Lost and found
I lost it.
Saw red.
Got angry.
Tried to even the score.

I lost it.
Saw fit
to take the law
into my own hands.

I lost it,
and in the process,
lost all sense of
what is right.

I lost it,
lashed out
and lost
my dignity.

I lost it,
and lost out.
But looking back,
I discovered one thing:

when I was lost
I found myself
searching
for you.

Unbreakable bonds of friendship

1 Samuel 20

Jonathan said to David, 'Whatever you want me to do, I'll do for you.' (4)

When the going is tough we all need someone dependable at our side. David found such a faithful friend in Jonathan, the eldest son of Saul and heir to the throne of Israel. Their friendship began after David had killed Goliath, which action filled Jonathan with admiration for the brave shepherd. Jonathan was also a soldier of valour, as was demonstrated in his victory over the Philistines on the night when he attacked them in their stronghold at Geba, accompanied by only his armour-bearer. Some years later David extolled Jonathon's courage in his lament for his fallen friend (2 Sam. 1:22), when he died at his father's side.

Throughout the chapters devoted to David's time in the court of Saul the reader is reminded of the strength of the relationship between him and Jonathan. Immediately after David had finished his conversation with Saul following his slaying of Goliath, '... *Jonathan became one in spirit with David, and he loved him as himself*' (1 Sam. 18:1). When David entered into Saul's service as both a minstrel in his court and a military leader with his army, Jonathan made a covenant with David, giving him his robe, tunic and weapons (1 Sam. 18:3, 4). Before long King Saul became increasingly jealous of David, until his anger turned into paranoia, at which point Jonathan had to decide between loyalty to his father and his devotion to David. He refused to take part in carrying out his father's plot to kill David with his father's attendant, and took a further step in warning his friend.

He was also prepared to stand by his friend, speaking well of him to Saul: *'Let not the king do wrong to his servant David; he has not wronged you, and what he has done has benefited you greatly. He took his life in his hands when he killed the Philistine. The LORD won a great victory for all Israel, and you saw it and were glad. Why then would you do wrong to an innocent man like David by killing him for no reason?'* (19:4–5). Jonathan could not have been more forthright in addressing his father, but Saul was in no mood to listen to reason. When the Spirit of the Lord departs a person, that individual is not left in a neutral state but is open and vulnerable to evil spirits taking over to cause increasing darkness in the soul.

David, who now finds himself banished from court, stood in even greater need of his friend's help. At the same time David was aware that Jonathan's position was made even more precarious by his continuing friendship, and that Saul's anger could so easily turn against his own son. A paranoid person sees everyone as a potential enemy. Jonathan, for his part, not only had to calm the suspicions of his father, but at the same time had to reassure David (9). Sometimes friendship demands a high price.

Jonathan promised to report to David his father's intentions towards him. This was a make-or-break time in their relationship and an appropriate moment to renew their mutual commitment. *'So Jonathan made a covenant with the house of David, saying, "May the LORD call David's enemies to account." And Jonathan made David reaffirm his oath out of love for him, because he loved him as he loved himself'* (16, 17).

To what extent are we prepared to enter into commitments of life-long friendship? Are we prepared to stand by another person, even when it is against our own interests? In doing so, Jonathan prefigured the self-giving love of Jesus.

A verse to remember: 'This is how we know what love is: Jesus Christ laid down his life for us. And we ought to lay down our lives for our brothers' (1 John 3:16).

Thanks to you
It's hard to accept
when people do good
things for you with
no strings attached.

It's easier, maybe,
when you believe
you'd be the first
to do the same –

or at least, you'd like
to think you would.
It's not always possible
to reciprocate

the extravagance of
a real sacrifice; but then you
died so that I wouldn't have to,
and the best way I can

possibly show how
grateful I am is to
choose to live
for you, with you

and always
thanks
to you,
my friend.

The most incredible
thing is that you've never
acted like you've got a
Cross to bear.

day 20 | Dealing with difficult people

1 Samuel 25:1–44

David said to Abigail, 'Praise be to the Lᴏʀᴅ, the God of Israel, who has sent you today to meet me. May you be blessed for your good judgment and for keeping me from bloodshed this day and from avenging myself with my own hands.' (32, 33)

David is far from being the hero of today's incident. That honour goes to Abigail, the wife of Nabal, an ill-tempered, mean and ungrateful man who had succeeded in making David see red, and of precipitating David's decision to embark on a violent course of action. It was Abigail's good sense and prompt action that prevented a needless blood bath.

Before we enter into the details of the story we pause to reflect on our own reactions to difficult people who seem so unreasonable and mean spirited. Some unpleasant individuals have the capacity to rile everyone with whom they have dealings. How do we respond when we are rubbed up the wrong way? Are there people whom we know will bring out the worst in us if we allow them to get under our skin? Servants do not have the luxury of choosing their associates nor those to whom they are accountable or on whom they depend.

These annoying individuals are in the habit of turning up just at the wrong moment to catch us off guard. On this occasion, David was feeling vulnerable because he had just lost his mentor and elder statesman, the prophet Samuel. He had also been worn down both physically and emotionally by the remorseless opposition of King Saul. Although David shows great magnanimity towards Saul, because he continued to regard him as 'the Lord's anointed', he could not muster the same forgiving spirit towards Nabal. David had reached the limit of his endurance.

David lived in lawless times due to a weak, capricious king and the constant Philistine threat. Bands of robbers roamed the countryside who found livestock easy pickings, because the lone shepherds who guarded them could be intimidated readily. David and his six hundred men provided protection for Nabal's goatherds and shepherds without asking payment. But this was no protection racket – from the story it is clear that Nabal's servants welcomed David and his men, regarding them as both friendly and honest. Their protectors did not take a single animal, either in payment or by way of dishonest gain. David and his men for their part had no alternative but to live off the land, so the arrangement was mutually beneficial.

The time of year for the goats and sheep to be sheared was traditionally a time of celebration and festivity. Rich people were expected to act with generosity towards the community at large, and especially towards those who had been of service. It was not unreasonable for David and his men to expect Nabal to show kindness in return for the protection they had provided for the animals now being sheared. They felt that one good turn deserved another in a culture where relationships were built and needs met by reciprocation.

But Nabal (literally 'fool') responds with a mean spirit. He was the kind of individual who thought only of himself, taking everyone else for granted, including his wife. His response to David's request showed not a hint of gratitude. His sneering remarks dismissed David as a good-for-nothing, runaway servant. He made no attempt to sound out his own servants to discover their assessment of David. Fools are not prepared to listen to reason, preferring to form their own opinions without stopping to consider the facts.

The unreasonableness of Nabal's attitude pushed David over the edge. Being unfairly described as an outlaw raised David's ire, especially as he had done all in his power to maintain good relationships with the paranoid king Saul. Stung by his wounded pride he retaliated without pausing to consider the wisdom or the justice of his actions. Rage has a blinding effect, so that things we do in the heat of the moment we later regret.

David was determined to convince himself of the justice of his response. He complained to himself and anyone within earshot (21, 22). But if he had stopped to think with a cool head he would have realized his quarrel was not with the servants but with Nabal. Such was the over-reaction of his temper tantrum. Retaliation has the habit of turning us into the enemy we despise.

Fortunately, Abigail, Nabal's beautiful and intelligent wife, intervened to prevent the impending blood bath. It is ironic that one of Nabal's servants, whom David was preparing to slaughter, had gone to Abigail to report how her husband had insulted David.

Abigail showed herself to be level headed, resourceful and tactful in responding promptly to the situation. Acting on her own initiative, and gathering supplies to placate David and as evidence of her good will towards him, she set off to intercept him. Meeting him while David was voicing his complaints to his men, Abigail gave the longest recorded speech of any woman in the Bible, beginning by diverting the blame from her husband to herself and informing David that she knew her husband only too well. *'May my lord pay no attention to that wicked man Nabal. He is just like his name – his name is Fool, and folly goes with him'* (25). We are left wondering why she, such an intelligent and resourceful woman, had married him in the first place? Had he changed over the years? Was it an arranged marriage? Whatever the explanation, she was stuck with him. Nabal was just not worth the drastic action that David had determined to carry out. As for his servants, they had suffered constantly under Nabal's cruel tongue lashing, whereas David had only suffered just one blistering encounter. And these were the very people that David was going to make suffer on account of their master.

When we are tempted to over-react in the face of needless provocation we too need someone with Abigail's qualities to help us see sense and to restrain our impetuosity. Or perhaps God would have us perform a similar service from time to time. In her approach to David we see her impressive demonstration of tact – she was prepared to take the blame in order to divert David's attention from his intended victim. She gently nudged David to re-examine the wisdom and justice of his actions. Her expressed desire not to cause offence indicated that she realized full well the delicacy of her mission, and that her approach could easily backfire.

Her magnanimous attitude was demonstrated not only by the generous gift that she brought but also in her sincere wishes for David. In contrast to her husband who represented David as an outlaw, she regarded him as one who was fighting the Lord's battles. She was here using flattery as a ploy in order to demonstrate the contrast between the good reputation she knew David would like to have had from the one that his cruel actions would have left him with. She anticipated the success of her mission by representing her intervention as the Lord's will to keep David from avenging himself through violent action.

And her strategy worked! She was instrumental in snapping David out of his dark mood to see things in a clear light for which he gave profound praise to God. *'Praise be to the Lord, the God of Israel, who has sent you today to meet me. May you be blessed for your good judgment and for keeping me from bloodshed this day and from avenging myself with my own hands'* (32).

The Bible makes it clear that we should leave our vindication in the hands of God, rather than attempt to play God. For the Lord has a way of working things out in his own way and time. The conclusion of this story is a case in point.

Abigail had made such an impression on David that he promptly asked her to marry him. Her response reflected her humble disposition, that she was ready not only to serve David, but also to become a servant to his servants. In accepting his proposal she entered into yet another unhappy household, although apparently she had the sense to keep clear of the family intrigues that caused so much distress for David in his old age.

Do you have the same courage, good sense, and tact in order to confront someone who has embarked on a course of destructive action that they will live to regret?

Hot head

How many times must I say
sorry? Why do I always seem
to lose it? I'm only human,
But that's no longer
An excuse. Any child of Yours
Is never 'only' anything, after all.

I'm sorry to be indignant
when I know I don't have a leg
To stand on. Let him without sin
cast the first aspersions ...
I find myself looking for splinters
in other people's eyes

When I can't see the wood
for the trees. Don't get right,
get even, they say. But even
if I could, what good would it do?
There's no such thing as even,
anyway; just a chain reaction that

keeps going and going, ripples
in a pond spreading outwards,
dominos falling and falling and
falling. Down. Help me to turn
a vicious circle into something of
virtue instead. Spreading outwards

like a conspiracy of hope;
choosing life at every turn,
turning from death to face up to
love, and however many times
it takes, finding the grace to say
I'm sorry.

day 21 | Prepared to be held accountable

2 Samuel 11 – 12:10

'As surely as the LORD lives, the man who did this deserves to die!' ... 'You are the man!' (12:5, 7)

Power has great destructive potency. Some ten years after taking up residence in Jerusalem David's personal life sank to an all time low. He succumbed to the corrupting notion that he could take whatever he wanted, whether possessions or people. Once again the Bible tells the story of the life of a servant with undisguised frankness.

This is a cautionary episode that does not lack for modern parallels among God's servants who have fallen into disgrace on account of lust and the ruthlessness that so often accompanies it. When we are in a relatively calm and stress-free situation we wonder why those who have been so godly and so wise would stray so far. But pressure that becomes unbearable and relentless can result in lonely servants developing a fantasy world as a way of escape, until eventually they find themselves living out those fantasies. This is borne out by the disturbing evidence of a significant number of church leaders who have become addicted to Internet pornography. Jesus makes the point that to look lustfully means that we have already committed adultery in our heart (Matt. 5:27, 28). The greater the life pressures that exert themselves upon us, the greater the power of the temptations we are likely to encounter. It does not take much to knock over a work-weary person.

On that fateful day, David had decided not to accompany his army into battle, even though it had been his usual practice, as well as being expected. Was his distance and detachment an indication that he was physically and emotionally drained? For whatever reason, on this occasion he sent others out to fight his battles. Taking a stroll on the roof of his palace, David discovered that temptations often come suddenly. He found himself gazing at a woman bathing on a nearby rooftop. He could not avoid the first glance but his mistake was in continuing to spy on her and indulge his imagination. Martin Luther commented that while we cannot prevent birds flying over our head, we could stop them nesting in our hair!

David made the first move, driven not by curiosity, but by lust. The information that she was the daughter of Eliam and the wife of Uriah the Hittite should have served to curb his cravings, for Eliam was the son of his most trusted counsellor Ahitophel, and her husband Uriah was a member of David's handpicked bodyguard. Consequently, his advances towards Bathsheba betrayed the loyalty of those who served him so faithfully. In taking her, David broke the sixth commandment in giving in to lust, the seventh in committing adultery, which in turn led to his breaking the tenth when he arranged Uriah's murder. Each of these violations carried the death penalty according to Old Testament law. There is no indication that Bathsheba, for her part, resisted his advances. The pleasures of a moment are enjoyed in disregard for the long-term consequences.

We go to extraordinary lengths to satisfy our cravings. When we allow ourselves to be driven by our emotions, they gather momentum, like a vehicle without brakes accelerating down a steep hill. The only safe thing to do is to take evasive action at the outset. We realize that lust is never satisfied and the law of diminishing returns drives us to seek increasingly powerful stimuli.

Upon discovering that Bathsheba was pregnant, David planned a cover-up, for Uriah would know that he couldn't possibly have fathered the child and that David was the culprit. So David decided to recall Uriah from the battlefront in order to provide opportunity for him to enjoy a gourmet meal followed by a romantic evening with his wife. But much to David's consternation, Uriah declined his king's offer with a declaration of loyalty that was in sharp contrast to David's treachery. Uriah insisted on sleeping at the door of the king's palace, refusing to be diverted from the task in hand. So David attempted to overcome Uriah's reluctance by getting him drunk – but this scheme proved equally unsuccessful.

David then instructed Joab, the commander of the army, to

abandon Uriah in the face of the enemy in order to bring about his death. By this action, David also implicated Joab in his sin, which further compounded his guilt. When the news of Uriah's death reached David his cynical response is a further indication of the hardened state of his heart: *'Don't let this upset you; the sword devours one as well as another'* (11:25) was his off-handed comment.

By this terrible act, the seriousness of which he had tried to shrug off, David had brazenly violated God's laws and shamelessly abused his royal power. After just seven days following her husband's death Bathsheba married David. But God knew, and the chronicler had no hesitation in declaring God's verdict: *'the thing David had done displeased the LORD'* (11:27).

No servant of God is immune from temptation. Those who think that they would never commit David's sin are in the greatest peril. We all need to heed God's word constantly and to have someone at our side who is prepared to confront us and hold us accountable. At this sad period in his life, the greatest king of Israel, and the nation's greatest songwriter, displeased, despised and utterly scorned the Lord. The narrative leaves us in no doubt about the seriousness of his actions. Yet at the same time his failure need not have been final, for there is a way back to God from the dark paths of sin.

God sent the prophet Nathan to hold David to account. Prophets are people who have learned to listen to God's voice and have the courage to confront. The mark of a true friend is someone who tells us what we need to hear, not just want we want to hear. Wisely, Nathan adopts an indirect approach in order to gain a hearing and to penetrate the king's evasive defensiveness.

The story Nathan told attracted David's sympathy and he burned with anger – but by his reaction he had hoisted himself on his own petard. He stood self-condemned as the villain in the story, at which point Nathan confronts his king directly: *'You are the man'* (12:7). David was held personally responsible for his death.

Sometimes ministry goes beyond counselling and teaching to issuing a direct challenge. We are reminded that there are absolute moral standards that are clear-cut and non-negotiable. An attitude of non-judgmental love must not be stretched to the point where anything goes. *'Why did you despise the word of the LORD by doing what is evil in his eyes?'* (12:9). The prophet's rebuke was followed by an announcement of divine judgment: *'... the sword shall never depart from your house'* (12:10). And so it turned out – eventually David was driven from Jerusalem by his son Absalom's conspiracy to seize the kingship.

Crashed

You were a sight for sore eyes,
a vision of beauty and colour
in a world of black and white.

You served to remind me that
I was red-blooded and deserved better
than to be pegged back by responsibility.

I basked in the glow of a
friendly screen, as I flickered
back into what I thought was life.

Turning on to you, a file to be downloaded,
dumped in acres of empty memory
and summoned every night when I heard the call.

How was I to know that my fantasy
would gatecrash reality? That I would
dream into being a life that no one wanted?

What might have been? I am left
with an empty screen and a broken drive.
One thing leads to another, they say,

and this one thing led me to you,
far away from home. Having served myself, I now
serve others once more ... but sadly as a warning.

way to
serve

part 5

Jesus and company

The Servant among servants

Sent out to serve

Luke 10:1–24

... the Lord appointed seventy-two others and sent them two by two ahead of him to every town and place where he was about to go (1)

In the Gospels, when mention is made of the disciples, we tend to think only of the Twelve whom Jesus called and whose names are recorded. But if we look more closely we soon find that there were many more disciples who remained nameless. For instance, early in Jesus' ministry John recorded in his Gospel that *'The Pharisees heard that Jesus was gaining and baptising more disciples than John'* (John 4:1). Their apprehension may have exaggerated their claim, but the biblical account testifies to the fact that John the Baptist was attracting large crowds drawn from many parts of the country. Also John records that after the miraculous feeding of the crowd of five thousand people, *'many of his disciples turned back and no longer followed him'* (John 6:66) – they were put off by his teaching.

Here in Luke's Gospel, we learn about the Seventy disciples of Jesus (or seventy-two, depending on the ancient source) who were sent ahead as he journeyed through Samaria from Galilee to Jerusalem. These Seventy disciples were additional to the Twelve. Whereas the Twelve are Apostles, i.e. 'sent ones', in a unique sense the entire church is also sent into the world on an ongoing apostolic mission. Seventy is a highly symbolic number of completeness, and also suggests the seventy nations that, according to Jewish tradition, represented the peoples of the world. Thus we may 'decode' Luke as communicating the message of the whole church going into the entire world at the command of Jesus as his representatives.

Matthew, Mark and John recorded the previous mission of the Twelve as compared with the mission of the Seventy, which is only reported by Luke. Where did this larger group come from? We have no additional information other than that which Luke here supplies. We do not even know their names. However, the pre-mission briefing given to them by Jesus was almost identical for both groups, but with the addition of an opening exhortation, *'The harvest is plentiful, but the workers are few. Ask the Lord of the harvest, therefore, to send out workers into his harvest field'* (2). Here is a reminder that the task would always be larger than one group could handle.

Those sent out were to bring the fruit of their preaching to Jesus, and not claim it for themselves. In response to the extent and urgency of the needs that surrounded Jesus' servants, they are ordered to pray for more labourers. Servants are best recruited through prayer rather than pressed into service as reluctant volunteers. And there is no excuse for a martyr complex whereby we refuse all offers of help, insisting on guarding our position jealously.

Jesus was frank about the dangers involved in the mission on which they were about to embark. They would become as vulnerable as helpless lambs among fierce wolves. But their response when threatened with attack was to call upon the Lord. Their reassurance rested on the one who had commissioned them: *'I am sending you out'* (3). Herein lay their protection. Furthermore, they were not to go alone but in pairs, both for mutual encouragement and assistance in the face of danger, as well as to reinforce their witness by giving it the authority required by the Jewish law.

Their vulnerability was expressed in yet another way. They were expressly forbidden to take with them a purse for money or a bag to carry food and were not permitted to have a spare pair of sandals, or possibly were even expected to travel barefoot. They were to journey in faith.

These strict instructions cannot be transferred in detail to every subsequent mission. The later missionaries of the early church worked for their support and received gifts to enable them to continue their ministries without reliance on those they were seeking to win to Christ. However, there is a general principle that applies in every situation, namely, that mission in Christ's name must always be undertaken in reliance upon the Lord and not simply in our own resources.

The Lord's further command may seem rather odd when read outside of its cultural context. His order, not to greet anyone on the road, should not be interpreted as a command to rudely ignore people they met along the way. Rather Jesus was making the point that they were not to dawdle and waste time because their task was urgent. Oriental greetings could be lengthy and time-consuming and they had to keep ahead of Jesus, ensuring that they didn't delay his progress. Also, this command must be balanced by the greetings that they were required to bring to the households they visited. The mission in question is an itinerant mission rather than a settled local ministry. Some people need to keep on the move for that is their distinctive calling.

The Seventy servants of Christ came to each household bringing a gift of peace, which is a Jewish way of referring to salvation. Their very presence brought a sense of well-being. To be received by a *'man of peace'* (6) meant to be received by a believer – someone

In any age it is all too easy for the church to become side-tracked with socializing rather than advance the mission with which it has been entrusted. Are you 'on track'?

whose heart God had prepared to receive their message. The people who gladly received them found benefit in being in their company to the extent that hospitality was spontaneously offered. To a welcome guest we say, 'You must stay. We will not hear of you going elsewhere.' But the gift had to be willingly received. It must not be imposed on the unresponsive or the ungrateful. And if people rejected them they would be the worse for it in that a rejected blessing became a curse. Faith is required in order to receive a blessing; it is not automatically conferred.

We must also bear in mind that the mission of both the Twelve and of the Seventy was not identical with Christian mission now; their mission took place when Jesus came as the long-expected Messiah to God's covenant people. That is why there is also a strong message of judgment against the communities that reject their message. If they were not welcomed they were to declare, *'Even the dust of your town that sticks to our feet we wipe off against you'* (11). This was a traditional saying that referred to a Jewish response to hostile Gentiles. Here it was applied to fellow Jews. Jesus' declaration of judgment singles out Korazin, Bethsaida and Capernaum (13–15) – the people of those towns had ample opportunity to hear his teaching and witness his miracles because they were located at the centre of his Galilean ministry. Yet they still rejected him. Sometimes familiarity can breed contempt.

Luke provides no account of the ministry of the Seventy, for his focus throughout is on the ministry of Jesus himself. But, on completing their mission assignment, they reported back to Jesus, rejoicing at the evidences they had seen of the power of God at work in breaking the hold of demonic power as they had ministered in Jesus' name. Jesus redirected their enthusiasm, cautioning that they should be rejoicing over what God had done in the lives of other people rather than in the power released through their ministry. They should rather rejoice that their names were written in heaven (20).

Jesus rejoiced in the way that God had revealed himself through the disciples, whom he described as *'little children'* (21), in contrast to the learned scribes and religious leaders. They had been given *'authority to trample on snakes and scorpions'* (19), creatures that were traditional symbols of evil. Jesus assured them of protection from the backlash of the power of the enemy. They had been privileged to see the signs of the Kingdom present as they had ministered in Jesus' name. It was through Jesus' teaching, and his relationship with his heavenly Father, that his disciples came to know the Father.

Those who had been sent out to bless others were themselves blessed as a result of their obedience (23–24). Such is the great reward and enormous privilege of servants who are obedient.

Over familiar

I could get used to this.
Freedom. Truth. Beauty.
It's not every day, after all, that you meet God.
No need to fear, he says.

Your past is forgiven, he says.
Wipe the slate clean, he says.
Start again.

It's like every Christmas and birthday
rolled into one.
Feeling like a new me,
recreated, regenerated, revitalized.
Seeing the world from another angle,
from upside down and inside out.
It all looks so different.
It all feels so different.

The trouble is,
I could get used to this;
please don't let me.

day 23 | Misguided ambition

Matthew 20:20-28

You don't know what you are asking ... (22)

Most of us are prone to take in only what we want to hear. We filter out the remainder, whether on purpose or unintentionally. Although the disciples had been hanging back in apprehension as they had followed Jesus on his climactic journey to Jerusalem, their hopes rose when they finally arrived – for they believed that the Kingdom that Jesus had said was at hand was now about to appear. That being the case, they reasoned that it was important for them to establish their own position in the power structure. During the journey south they had been arguing among themselves who would be the greatest in the kingdom. Overhearing them, Jesus had made it clear, '... *whoever wants to become great among you must be your servant, and whoever wants to be first must be slave of all'* (Mark 10:43–44). And since that was something they didn't want to hear, they filtered it out.

Soon after arriving in Jerusalem, the brothers James and John stole a march on the other disciples. They persuaded their mother to ask a favour on their behalf. And like any Jewish mother who is ambitious and outspoken on behalf of her sons, she was only too willing to oblige. An older woman could get away with asking more than the disciples felt able to. Jesus invited her to say exactly what she wanted on behalf of her sons, so she came straight to the point, *'Grant that one of these two sons of mine may sit on your right and the other at your left in your kingdom'* (Matt. 20:21). When we are explicit about our ambitions, our motives are laid bare as well as the limits of our understanding.

The overriding desire of this strong willed pair, known for their short fuses, was wrong headed to the point of embarrassment. But at least it revealed that they were not ready to 'jump ship', for they still believed in Jesus and his intention to establish his Kingdom. However, not for the first time, they, like the other disciples, revealed their failure to grasp the true nature of the Kingdom of God. By requesting to sit on either side of him they were not expressing their desire for intimacy but were declaring their bid for power. They were moved, not by loyalty, but by misguided ambition that was not only wrong-headed but also wrong-hearted. To put it crudely, they considered it as 'pay back' for their sacrificial commitment. They felt that leadership should consist of a life of privilege, prestige and power. Moreover, their sudden move would ensure that Andrew and Peter did not stake a prior claim.

Jesus told the brothers and their mother that they did not know what they were asking. *'Can you drink the cup I am going to drink?'* (20:22) he asked them. And their reply was immediate and self-assured, *'We can.'* No questions asked. They clearly had in mind the cup of joyful celebration, not realizing that Jesus was referring to the cup of suffering, which he himself could hardly bear the thought of drinking. In fact, Jesus would soon sweat blood at the thought while on his knees pleading with his heavenly Father in the Garden of Gethsemane to remove the cup (Matt. 26:42). As for the brothers, they would

Are you prepared to ask and then pay the price of servant-style leadership in the name of Jesus?

also both drink the cup of suffering in due course: James was arrested ten years later by King Herod and put to death with the sword; sixty years later, John was in exile on the isle of Patmos.

The places of power in the kingdom of God were not what they imagined. Furthermore, those two privileged positions were not for Jesus to give: *'These places belong to those for whom they have been prepared'* (23) he told them. Jesus knew the limits of his own authority. The irony was that in Jesus' moment of triumph on the cross, those on his right and left were two robbers, and one of those would be the first into the Kingdom!

Both symbols, the baptism and the cup, emphasize the cost of following Christ. Baptism represented initiation into the death and resurrection of Christ, and the cup of wine symbolized participation in the new Covenant through the shedding of Christ's blood. His

sacrificial death secured our forgiveness, assured us of our reconciliation and anticipated the joyful celebration of his second coming to
earth to consummate his Kingdom. Only those who suffer with him
will reign with him.

The unwelcome initiative of James and John triggered an
immediate response from the other disciples – they were indignant,
not because they felt their request was unreasonable but because
they considered James and John to be out of line. They realized that
they had been out-manoeuvred. The scene had turned ugly as the
power struggle amongst peers heightened tension. Such tension
breaks to the surface whenever there is a jostling for power,
particularly during a time of transition. Their request was evidence
that a servant spirit has been displaced by a desire to gain power and
control.

Jesus intervened, calling his servants to order. And his rebuke was
not confined to James and John but directed at them all. He was well
aware they had repeatedly blocked out his predictions of his trial,
scourging and death on the Cross – and they had made clear their
misunderstanding of his teaching on the nature of the Kingdom. We,
like them, only hear what we want to hear, filtered according to our
expectations and desires. As on other occasions, Jesus' teaching
arises out of a specific context. When we learn on a need-to-know
basis we are much more likely to remember what we have been
taught.

Jesus challenged their concept of leadership by drawing a sharp
contrast to the leadership styles they had known over the centuries,
under the domination of the Babylonians, Persians, and now, for the
past twenty-five years, under the repressive authority of the Roman
army of occupation. Having been on the receiving end, did they now
want to turn into the perpetrators? Leadership in God's Kingdom was
very different. In the Jesus community greatness is measured by
service not by power, prestige and privilege. The first person among
them is not the individual at the top but the one at the bottom. This is
a principle Jesus not only preached but also practised. Although he
was the Son of Man sent from heaven he had not come to be served,

but to serve. His model of service was more costly than it could ever be for any other person; as the sinless Son of God he laid down his life as the price that must be paid to deliver those enslaved by sin. The burden he carried as a servant was not on behalf of a single person, but for the sins of the whole world. The only limitation is whether or not we are prepared to receive it and so be numbered among 'the many' (28).

Leadership through self-giving service was a hard lesson for Jesus' first followers to learn. They needed to be taught it repeatedly for that truth gradually to sink in. It is the same for those who follow nearly two thousand years later.

Priorities
What's that?

To be blind is to see?
To give is to get?
To lose is to find?
To be poor is to be rich?
To be last is to be first?
To lead is to follow?
To rule is to serve?

That's what.

A god who's dying for me to live.

day 24 | Devotion and duty

Luke 10:38-42

... you are worried and upset about many things, but only one thing is needed (41, 42)

Depending on our personality type, we either identify with Martha or with Mary in today's story. Among close friends, work colleagues and within marriages there is often a predictable tension produced by our varied responses to people and situations. Some individuals are task-oriented while others are people-focused. The social dynamics become entangled and heated through personality clashes when you live in a tight-knit community or work as a member of a team.

Experts in Myers–Briggs personality profiling analysis would label Martha as an 'SJ' (Sensing/Judging). People in this category tend to be readily responsive, noticing details and the realities of the here and now. They are steadfast, persistent, and insistent, with a keen awareness of what needs to be done, and a strong sense of obligation to get on with it without delay. Sometimes it is difficult for Martha-types to see beyond the immediate, but they play an important role by being prepared to 'roll up their sleeves' in serving others.

Mary's Myers–Briggs profile is probably that of an 'NF' (Intuitive/Feeling). Persons of this type look beyond the immediate, being concerned with the bigger picture. They are constantly relating events and ideas in order to discern the significance of the links that they have established. Mary-types are visionaries who become captivated by an idea but without necessarily knowing how to realize their vision and lacking patience to deal with the details. They are happiest in the world of ideas and especially in the presence of someone who can stimulate their thinking.

The setting for the incident is the town of Bethany, two miles from Jerusalem. Jesus had just arrived on the final leg of his long journey from Galilee when Martha and Mary welcomed him. Note that both sisters were enthusiastic about his visit. It was not a case of Martha responding begrudgingly and then finding something to complain about. She did not have a chip on her shoulder.

In fact it was Martha rather than Mary who apparently took the initiative in offering her home to the Lord. It is possible that Martha was a widow, which would have made her even more resolute in taking charge of the situation to compensate for the loss of her husband. As head of the household and a dutiful host, she considered it her personal responsibility to make sure that everything possible was done for Jesus.

It is not clear whether Jesus visited alone, or whether he was accompanied by any or all of his disciples. If the latter, then her domestic burden was even greater. Martha was aptly named, for 'Martha' means 'mistress'. In the service of Christ, Martha-types are of vital importance, otherwise, when faced with a decision, the response will be all talk but little action. We all know the truth of the saying, 'When all is said and done, too much is said and too little is done!'

On this occasion Jesus commended Mary for choosing to listen to him, and for refusing to allow Martha to deprive her of her golden opportunity, which was almost certainly her last. Bearing in mind that Jesus spent most of his time in the northern district of Galilee, she would have known few occasions when she could sit and learn from him. Another important consideration is that Jesus was unique among the rabbis in welcoming women among his disciples and providing them with the occasion to receive his teaching. Consequently, Mary was determined to grasp the chance when it was presented to her.

Her sister's different ordering of priorities, which, in her view, were misplaced, annoyed Martha. She was so obsessed with the meal arrangements that she had no time to stop and listen. She had become *'distracted by all the preparations'* (40) to the point that she had become overwhelmed by anxiety and could not stop fussing. No matter how much she did there was always something else she felt needed her attention. Such an important guest was deserving of the very best, but things had gotten out of proportion to the point where everyone around her was on edge.

Jesus' message to Martha was that she had allowed her preparations to become too burdensome. He had not come to be entertained with an elaborate meal but rather to spend time with them to share what was on his heart. He would be content with a far simpler meal to maximize their time together.

The problem of identifying too closely with either the Martha or the Mary camps is that in so doing we fail to recognize the strengths of the other side. We need both the doers and the thinkers. But one must not act in isolation from the other, or with little concern for the pressures that the other might be facing. In the story Martha became increasingly agitated, until she blurted out her complaint to her guest, *'Lord, don't you care that my sister has left me to do all the work by myself? Tell her to help me!'* (40). It is difficult to believe that Jesus was unaware of the tension that had developed in the room. He could hardly have failed to notice Martha scurrying around.

With whom do you most identify and what have you learned from this incident?

From Martha's complaint we must not assume that Mary was an impractical dreamer, or that her 'spirituality' was a smokescreen for laziness. The fact that Martha complained that Mary had 'left her' implies that earlier she had been doing her share of the work. On the other hand, it is likely that nothing would have been ready on time if everything had been delegated to Mary! The point of the story is not to persuade us all to be contemplative in temperament, but to emphasize that there is a time to put down our utensils, wipe her hands, take some deep breaths and to give Jesus our full and undivided attention.

The underlying issue was not business but distractedness. Martha-types are prone to want Jesus to deal with matters as they define them, rather than allowing the Lord to deal with us on his terms. Duty must be balanced by devotion. Unrelenting service will eventually wear us down to the point where we become disgruntled and finally exhausted. Those who find great personal satisfaction in serving others must themselves recognize their personal need of ministry.

Jesus was determined to gain Martha's attention with the repetition of her name, *'Martha, Martha'* (41). He is concerned for her as a person who had her own needs, which he would not allow her to cover up or avoid by her business. There are moments when *'only one thing is needed'*.

When the Lord seeks to gain our attention we ignore his invitation at our peril. In the church today there are faithful workers who are always busy doing this and that. There are compulsive workers who are always ready to give but who resist receiving from others, thereby turning into brittle personalities. Eventually, when some crisis hits, some deep disappointment, some grave moral problem, some incapacitating or life-threatening disease, they may then discover that they do not have the spiritual resources to cope with the situation. Furthermore, they are prone to cut themselves off from those who reach out to help them. This is because they would not give the time to listen and to learn over the course of the years.

This story challenges us to keep our priorities clear. We need to avoid the tyranny of the urgent that so persistently crowds out the significant, if we allow it to. Fruitfulness does not come from frenzy but from faithfulness in hearing God's word, retaining it and in translating it into action. In the first place we pray, 'Lord, make me a listener'; then, 'make me a worshiper'; and, lastly, 'make me a worker'.

Driven to Distraction

They say I'm driven.

Purposeful, task-orientated,
I get things done.
I'm a problem solver,
a go getter,
a die-hard, live fast
bleed-it-dry, non-stop
human dynamo.

Do it yourself,
that's what I say.
If a job's worth doing,
it's worth doing well.
But then, there's always another one
appearing on the radar.
As soon as you've finished
painting the Forth Bridge,
you need to start again.
It's like Sisyphus,
rolling his boulder up the hill
until he gets to the top –
aching, straining, labouring
to finish the task, until
it rolls down the other side
and he has to start all over again.

The poor will always be with you,
Jesus said. But I won't be.
Which seems a little harsh.

I wish I had time to stop
and think about that,
but I must press on, or

I'll be driven to distraction.

| Serving with humility

John 13:1–17

Jesus knew that the Father had put all things under his power,
and that he had come from God and was returning to God; so he
got up from the meal, took off his outer clothing, and wrapped a
towel around his waist (3, 4)

There are some past events in life we would not want to revisit. They
were significant at the time but we have moved on since then. In
contrast there are other occasions we need to revisit and ponder
afresh because we missed so much of what was said that we were not
able to understand at the time. The upper room conversation that
Jesus had with his closest followers was just such an occasion. The
first disciples of Jesus needed to return to that experience in the light
of subsequent events. We too can profit by replaying and considering
carefully what happened and what was said on that occasion. In
recognition of the importance of all that transpired in the upper room
during Jesus' final hours on earth, we will devote the next five days
to that one occasion.

As Jesus' ministry reached its climax, the *Sent One* becomes the
Sending One. His class of learners was about to become his apostolic
mission team. The fact that these servants were to be appointed as
messengers entrusted with the Good News of Jesus and his Kingdom
surfaces throughout the narrative. During this time of transition the
disciples' apprehension and self-doubt was revealed in the questions
raised by Peter, Thomas, Philip and Judas.

Even as they arrived in the Upper Room they continued to
manoeuvre for position despite the fact that their preconception
concerning the nature of the Kingdom had been shattered in the
aftermath of Jesus' triumphal entry into Jerusalem. They could not
compute what Jesus was now saying to them for they were too
disturbed and distressed.

Our meditations on these five chapters will focus on five issues
that are just as basic to our participation in Jesus' mission as they

were for his first century servants: serving, trusting, abiding, enduring and sending. First, 'serving with humility':

Throughout the Gospel narrative Jesus modelled a style of servant leadership that could never be interpreted as demeaning servitude. As the Servant of the Lord, Jesus was primarily responsible to his heavenly Father, with whom he maintained the most intimate of relationships. Both the dignity and contentment of the servant depends upon the person being served. At that moment in his life, *'Jesus knew that the time had come for him to leave this world and go to the Father'* (1). The word translated 'hour' has a special ring to it, alerting the reader that Jesus had a deep and profound awareness that he had arrived at a significant time, a hinge moment. In serving the Lord, remaining in tune and being on time are key elements in decision-making.

Jesus was first and foremost the servant of his heavenly Father. He allowed neither the crowds nor his followers to determine his agenda. Throughout his life he exercised 'prophetic freedom', for if he had simply responded to the urgent needs that people brought to him, he would never have left Galilee, where he was in so much demand, to *'resolutely set out for Jerusalem'* (Luke 9:51).

We learn from John's account that serving is unconditional. Jesus *'... loved his own who were in the world, ... [and] showed them the full extent of his love'* (13:1). His love for them is mentioned thirty-nine times during the upper room discourse. He loved them completely, despite their shortcomings, their lack of understanding, their questionable motives, and their eventual betrayal, denial and desertion. Jesus was also aware that since his arrival in Jerusalem with his disciples, Judas had been plotting his betrayal to the authorities.

When we read in John's account that *'Jesus knew that the Father had put all things under his power, and that he had come from God and was returning to God ... '* (3), I wonder what we would have anticipated coming next, following on from such a lofty statement? We might have expected reference to his seeking solitude, or for him to ask his disciples to provide some special need he had before he departed. But the unexpected happened. He *'got up from the meal, took off his outer clothing, and wrapped a towel around his waist'* (4).

Jesus was never too preoccupied to undertake a practical task. Serving entails taking the initiative: if something needs to be done, we should move into action without waiting to be asked or ordered. There in the upper room, the rented accommodation where Jesus and his disciples were gathered for a meal, everyone present must have been aware that there was no household servant to remove the dirt from their feet. Presumably the towel had been placed where every-one could see it, but everyone avoided noticing. No one was prepared to make the first move. Foot washing was considered a task so menial that no Jewish slave owner could order a Jewish slave to wash the feet of another Jew. Yet performing such lowly service was not beneath the dignity of Jesus.

Serving means being prepared to do anything – for it is love, not duty or intimidation, that motivates true service. What Jesus stooped to perform on that occasion was more than a humble service; it was an acted parable of the Lord's humiliation unto death. It was an indication of a deeper level of service. For within a few short hours his garments would be removed and he would stoop down to take up his Cross.

When the disciples realized what Jesus was about do, only Peter responded with an indignant outburst. His protest and overreaction arose from his embarrassment and pride. Perhaps he was also ashamed at the reluctance that he and the rest had shown in ignoring the towel. Like Peter, some of God's servants find it more difficult to receive than to give. They find personal satisfaction in service, doing it for their own benefit or to protest their own self-sufficiency. They find their identity in *doing* rather than in *being* and consequently resent any role reversal.

But willingness to be served by Jesus was not an option. Jesus cautioned Peter, *'Unless I wash you, you have no part with me'* (8).

> What is your greatest challenge? Being prepared to do anything, or resisting the pressure to do everything?

John's commentary on this incident points out that the significance of Jesus' words only became clear in the light of the Cross. Peter's devotion was defective in that it lacked humility. He then overacted in a manner typical of his impetuous personality: if his future relationship with Jesus was at stake then he was prepared to be washed all over! Peter had missed the point. Receiving forgiveness from Jesus for all our sins is a once and for all act of initiation. In baptism we are cleansed from sin, we share in Christ's death, and we rise to new life. After that we need a daily foot washing to remove the clinging dirt we collect as we walk through the world.

Service does not mean being pressured into doing everything. Herein lies the difference between wearing a towel and becoming a doormat. How many times did Jesus wear the towel? Only once! Service entails being prepared to do anything, however menial. It does not entail succumbing to the pressure to meet every demand that people try to heap upon us. Like Jesus we are primarily servants of the Lord. As such we are called to do his bidding, which at times will mean having the determination to say 'No' in response to people who make demands. Rather, everyone must be prepared to 'take up their towel' and play their part in the serving community.

What's the big idea?

You didn't get where you are today
by washing people's feet.
I hate to say it, but it doesn't become you,
stooping so low when you're reaching so high.
Down on your knees when others around you
should be down on theirs.

There's work to be done
and even though I say it myself,
you haven't got time to
waste on trivialities.
We're on a mission,
after all, and things are getting tough.

Come on! When the going gets tough,
the tough don't start washing feet,

do they?

I can see it all, almost as if I were
there once more. Nothing ever
seemed to fit with Jesus,
until it all fell into place.

What's the big idea? Where's this
all heading? Surely it'll end in tears
unless we get this thing
nailed?

Look where it got him, they said.
It got him all the way to us.

day 26 | Trusting in the midst of turmoil

John 13:36 – 14:31

Peace I leave with you; my peace I give you. I do not give to you as the world gives. Do not let your hearts be troubled and do not be afraid (14:27)

When things are going well it is all too easy for us to live with a false sense of security. We encounter little difficulty in trusting the Lord during times of tranquillity and predictable change. But as servants of the Lord, and of one another, we must survive in a climate characterized by uncertainty and the unexpected. During such disturbing times we may surprise ourselves by the unpredictability and strength of our own reactions. Upheavals bring out both the best – and the worst – in all of us.

Those leaders who want to be 'in command' find that their stress levels increase significantly as circumstances spiral out of their control. But for a true servant, to 'manage' does not mean to 'control' – it means 'to cope', which was the original meaning of the word. Coping signifies responding promptly and appropriately to meet the challenges of each new development. We learn to deal with our feelings of insecurity and apprehension in facing the unknown because of our trust in the Lord, who treated his close followers not as those from whom he demanded blind obedience, but as friends in whom he confided. One of the greatest challenges facing a servant is to continue to trust when our expectations have been shattered.

At this stage in the conversation in the Upper Room, Peter revealed not only his lack of understanding but also his insecurity. His question *'Lord, where are you going?'* (13:36) was anxiety driven. He wanted to be reassured that he would continue to know the comfort of Jesus' physical presence every step of the way, just like the past three years. Peter was not yet ready to confess his Lord in the face of rejection and ridicule, as his subsequent threefold denial showed. His continuing protests in response to Jesus' warnings revealed the need for his wilfulness to be broken, for he still relied too much on his own understanding and assessment of the situation. But we can find comfort and encouragement as we observe the Lord's patience with his servants, no matter how misguided and unprepared they revealed themselves to be.

As we learn to trust God in the course of stumbling through life, we are assured that we will meet God as we journey day by day. The early Celtic missionaries understood this truth. For them life was a pilgrimage, not to reach some distant destination where they would eventually enter some holy place, but to encounter the Lord in the course of their journey.

At every stage in life's journey we need to find places where we are welcomed and where we feel that we belong. The place that Jesus prepared for his disciples, and for all of his servants in every age, is not some Heavenly Hilton at **How would you describe the stage you are now at in your journey of faith?** the end of life's journey but is a series of wayside inns along our route. The Father's house is not a mansion in the sky, but represents our spiritual position in Christ, both now and for eternity. Jesus assured his disciples that there was room for all, with no one excluded. We each travel with room reservation numbers!

Furthermore, Jesus reassured his servants, *'If I go ... I will come back and take you to be with me that you also may be where I am'* (14:3). They would not be left to continue the journey of faith alone. Jesus described himself as *'the way, the truth and the life'* leading us to the Father (14:6). Getting there was not a matter of following directions, or reading a map, but walking with a guide.

Having observed Jesus closely for three years the disciples found Jesus to be *'full of grace and truth'* (John 1:14). In other words they knew him to be incredibly generous, completely genuine and utterly dependable. It is he alone who imparts *the life* from a fountain that never runs dry. Abundant life is not just having a good time, but consists in relating to God in the way that he intended. Notice the sequence: first, we must be prepared to walk the path of obedience; second, we must be ready to stand before the bar of truth which will unmask all of our pretence and wrong-headedness; and third, we must live the life that requires being prepared to die to self. Jesus invites us to robust and authentic living.

Philip now chimed in as a sincere seeker, but with limited understanding. He was looking for an experience. He demanded, *'Lord, show us the Father and that will be enough for us'* (14:8). It is difficult for us today to appreciate how revolutionary was Jesus' teaching about God as his heavenly Father. In Judaism there is scarcely a mention of God as Father. Many people have difficulty in trusting a father figure because of painful family memories of abdication, abandonment, or abuse by their earthly father. But rather than project on to God our experiences of fatherhood, we should derive our understanding of what it means to be a Father by learning from the life and teaching of Jesus. Here Jesus declared himself to be the perfect representation of God as Father.

Our confidence in him will be strengthened as we participate in the ministry of Jesus. He said that they would do *even greater works* because he was going to the Father (14:12). Whatever could he mean? Surely, not that we would do greater miracles of healing and deliverance, not to mention raising the dead? No, he had something even more significant in mind! For when Jesus had completed his saving work and sent his Holy Spirit, then his servants would see the greater fruits of his ministry in terms of transformed lives and in the impact on the world that the ever-increasing number of communities of Jesus would make. The gift of eternal life is even more dramatic than the gift of restored life. The latter is but a sign of the former.

His promise that he would do anything we ask in his name does not represent some magic formula. He is not providing a blank cheque. The limiting clause is in asking *'in his name'*, which signifies anything that is according to his character and purpose. It should never be considered as a means of getting our own way, but that the Father may be glorified through Jesus.

The disciples' confidence was also renewed through the promised

Holy Spirit. Here Jesus refers to the Counsellor (*Paraclete*) for the first time (14:16). His coming to us is conditional on our love for Jesus, demonstrated by our obedience to him. The Spirit comes as a *gift* bestowed by the Father in accordance with Jesus' request. The *Paraclete* is literally the 'one who comes alongside' to guide, encourage, empower and console. The Spirit will continue to do for Christ's servants precisely what Jesus had done for them on earth. That is why the Spirit is described as *another counsellor*, meaning not a different kind, but one of the same kind. We do well to remember that the work of the Spirit should never be divorced from that of the Father and the Son.

When Jesus departed they would not be abandoned as orphans, but would be adopted as sons through the Spirit. His presence that had been *with* them was about to be *in* them (17, 18). That was why it was to their advantage that he went away. We too are able to experience trust in the midst of turmoil precisely because we know the security provided by our spiritual adoption. Judas was confused because he was looking for Jesus to reveal himself afresh not only to them but to the world in some dramatic way; so he pleaded with Jesus to make everything turn out right without delay. But the way of Jesus was not to provide instant answers. Rather the disciples were called to live by faith, and peace would be the fruit of that trust (27). *Peace* signifies not tranquillity but a calm confidence in the midst of turmoil that is grounded in God rather then dependent on circumstances. Love is the foundation of peace that drives out fear.

Jesus did not want to talk any more for he must prepare himself for his last encounter with his Adversary, the ruler of this world. The time had come for Jesus to withdraw, but the disciples continued to linger. So Jesus set aside his personal agenda to continue to minister to them – such is the heart of the self-giving servant.

Going ahead
The Word became flesh and blood
and moved into the neighbourhood.

And the word is, God became a baby:
depended on others for food and water,
and maybe even love.

The word is, God learned to crawl,
just like any other normal child.

The word is, God took his first steps,
literally: as a toddler,
he set out on a journey.

The word is, God set out on the journey
of life itself. He learned to live.

And the word is that God has gone before us
Once again, to prepare the Way,
to make it straight.

As one journey ends, another begins,
and though we can't touch him,

The word is, he's with us in Spirit,
reaching out to touch us,
and teaching us to walk.

Abiding is the secret of fruitfulness

John 15:1–17

Remain in me, and I will remain in you. No branch can bear fruit ... unless you remain in me (4)

Whereas most people speak in terms of wanting to be successful, Jesus emphasizes that his servants should be *'fruitful'*. There is an important distinction between these two outcomes. Fruitfulness is the true test of the servant, because it means the reproduction and multiplication of the same kind of life. Jesus' own life was a powerful and challenging demonstration of that principle. He was indeed concerned with outcomes, but not couched in the language of success and achievement.

The fruit a tree bears identifies it unmistakably (Matt. 7:16). The fruit embodies the superabundance of life that the tree cannot contain within itself. It is the tree's give-away life. Fruitfulness inseparably relates quality and quantity. It makes us ask such questions as: 'What kind of an influence am I having on the people around me?' 'What kind of an atmosphere do I create when I enter a room?' 'What kind of a legacy am I leaving?'. In the church we are in the business of growing people into the likeness of Christ, to become people who will go out and make a difference in the world.

Wayne Jacobsen's book *In My Father's Vineyard* provides valuable insights in interpreting this extended metaphor as one who grew up in his father's vineyard. He points out that the branches are an integral part of the vine, not simply attached to it. There is no fixed line where the vine ends and the branch begins. Jesus wants us to identify so closely with him that others cannot tell where he leaves off and where we begin.

Jesus was not confining his remarks to individuals, but was addressing a community. In the Old Testament the nation of Israel was frequently referred to as a vine. The prophet Isaiah described

Israel as a *'vineyard'* planted and lovingly tended by God (Is. 5:1–7). The Psalmist praised God, *'You brought a vine out of Egypt; you drove out the nations and planted it. You cleared the ground for it, and it took root and filled the land'* (Ps. 80:8–9).

In declaring to his disciples, *'I am the true vine'* (1), Jesus was here drawing a contrast between himself and official Judaism. He was claiming to have come to create a new people, realizing God's intentions expressed long before in the Scriptures. The Gardener also comes to us to examine our lives, to inspect the fruit. What kind of harvest will he find in terms of quality and quantity? We are left in no doubt what kind of fruit God is looking for. Centuries before, the prophet Isaiah describes a previous inspection. *'The vineyard of the LORD Almighty is the house of Israel, and the men of Judah are the garden of his delight. And he looked for justice, but saw bloodshed; for righteousness, but heard cries of distress'* (Is. 5:7). God was not looking for *religious* people; he was looking for *righteous* people exhibiting the moral qualities of justice, self-control, fair dealing and compassion toward the needy. May God grant that the watching world will see those qualities clearly and consistently demonstrated through our corporate and personal lives.

How can this become increasingly true for us? How can we live fruitful lives? Jesus' teaching explains that we have to do two things (simply stated, but applying them will challenge us our entire lifetime): first, to abide in Christ; and second, to be prepared to submit to his pruning. *'If'* occurs five times in this passage as a caution that we have to participate actively in the life of the vine, for we can become easily distracted and preoccupied with other interests and concerns.

'Abiding' must be distinguished from *'hiding'*. It does not signify the avoidance of responsibility and not an invitation to become cowardly or lazy. It signifies a relationship rather than a refuge, meaning yielding to Christ's control and drawing our very life and sustenance from him. Bishop J. C. Ryle, a renowned bishop of Liverpool in the nineteenth century, paraphrased our Lord's command: 'Abide in me. Cling to me. Stick fast to me. Live your life of

close and intimate communion with me. Cast your whole weight on me. Never let go your hold on me for a moment ...'.

Jesus was here addressing his disciples. For them, *'abiding'* meant developing an already existing relationship. The same lesson applies to believers today. Sports people and other high achievers receive training in 'centring' their lives through meditation and visualization, in order to concentrate their energies to push their performance to a higher level. But Jesus goes deeper in the passage we are considering. He was speaking in spiritual rather than psychological terms. He was not laying a foundation to which the human potential movement can appeal to bolster its claims. Christianity it not a self-help programme that we can utilize and then discard at will in a journey towards self-realization. In contrast, the teaching of Christianity emphasizes the need to die to self in order to live the abundant life!

Fruitfulness comes from 'abiding'. What legacy do you want to leave?

Jacobsen makes the point that 'abiding' signifies 'remaining', which is repeated ten times in this passage. It entails demonstrating love for the long haul. The only difference between a cane and a branch is longevity. A cane is this season's growth, whereas a branch may be forty or more years old. Furthermore, these older branches not only channel life, they bear weight and multiply fruit. Abiding is not a changeless state of being, but a relationship that must be sustained through the changing seasons of life.

Jacobsen draws out the significance of the distinctive seasons in the growth cycle of the vine. Springtime is a period of rapid growth, but vines take their time. They are not the first to herald the spring. Although the growth of the vine is rapid it is vulnerable to adverse weather conditions and to weeds and pests. The new canes have to be trained to run along the supporting frame. We too may resist being bent against our will.

Next, the vines require summer heat to bring the fruit to maturity. This is a time for the maturing of the vine. During the hot summer months the vinedresser has to work hard with little to show for his backbreaking routines. But then summer gives way to autumn, the time for harvesting, which can also be an anxious time as the vinedresser is aware that his crop could be destroyed before he has had time to pick it. The vinedresser is concerned not only for the abundance of the crop but also for its quality in order to produce a good vintage as well as seed for planting to ensure future vines. Then comes winter, providing a welcome period for rest and re-staging. There are times in life when we have to learn to let go.

If we are beginning to think that abiding has a cosy ring to it, Jesus' second point will soon dispel that image. Abiding not only requires patience, it entails pain. Jesus wants us to *be* better and to *do* better. He is not content to leave us as we are so he trims the excess from our lives. Pruning is a drastic and painful process. Consequently, the amateur gardener tends to prune timidly for fear of damaging or killing off the plant. But the skilful professional is prepared to cut right back. It is a drastic process, which can appear very cruel at the time. God may use pain, sorrow, disappointment, or frustrated ambition to prune our lives. It is a paring back to essentials and entails cutting out the dead wood. The objective is not to increase foliage, but fruit: *'more fruitful ... much fruit'* (1, 5). The Lord is not being destructive but helping us to realize that there is a price to pay in order to become more productive. As with the gardener, that is seldom obvious at the time.

Some Christians believe that religion is to make them happy and contented rather than fruitful. Pruning provides a powerful test of the seriousness of their intentions. Do we really want to abide in Christ? Do we want to develop into a Christ-like character? Then pruning is an unavoidable part of the price we pay. Perhaps at this time you are experiencing a painful cutting back. Jacobsen comments that we sometimes feel that we are being cut through by a chain saw rather than cut back by a pruning knife. 'Lord how much more do we have to lose?' we wonder.

But when Jesus said, *'Abide in me'*, he wasn't asking us to stay and be pruned to the point that there is nothing left. In his hands the pruning always leads to fruitfulness, provided we learn to submit to it.

But what when the pruning ends in death? There is the supreme test of faith. As Christians we believe that life on this planet is an inconclusive experience. Our years here are but the preface to the fuller life. Fruitful living is a far more worthwhile lifetime goal than successful living.

All servants of Christ need to ask themselves: 'What do I want to be known for at the end of my life?' and 'How can I finish well?'. The secret of finishing well is to abide in Christ, and to submit to his pruning, no matter how painful. Fruitfulness is not the result of what we do, but is the outcome of who we are.

Branching out

I sometimes wonder whether I will like the old man
I am growing to become.

It seems a long way off, a trek along the journey.

But if I sat next to him on a bus,
would I see something of me
in his smile, in the book he was reading,
the clothes he was wearing?
Would I want to talk to him,
to learn from his wisdom,
the distillation of his years?
Would the lines on his face read like a map
of the paths of a life well-lived?

I would ask him how he'd wish to sum up his days:
his epitaph, to be gazed on by passers by
and watered by dogs. It should be clearer,
by then, what this young man was destined
to do, and who he was to become.

Perhaps, by then, thanks to the roots
I am growing now,
he will have branched out,

and borne fruit.

# day 28 | Enduring with confidence

John 15:18 – 16:4, 17–33

Remember the words I spoke to you: 'No servant is greater than his master.' If they persecuted me, they will persecute you also ... You will grieve, but your grief will turn to joy (15:20; 16:20)

Servants of God seeking to be faithful to their Lord should not be surprised when they encounter hostility in the world. We Christians in the West have been lulled into a sense of false security because of our 'Christendom' mentality, which historically has given the church a legitimized place in our culture. As Christendom has crumbled and given way to an increasingly neo-pagan cultural environment, western churches have not known how to respond appropriately. The extent and depth of our insecurity finds expression either in anger and indignation, feeling that our rights have been violated, or by silence and withdrawal as a defence against intimidation and ridicule. At such times we need to heed the Lord's words to his closest followers gathered in the Upper Room: *'If the world hates you, keep in mind that it hated me first'* (15:18).

However, we must not be too quick to assume that just because we are facing hostility in the home and workplace because of our Christian profession that God must be on our side. We may be disliked because of our judgmental attitudes, or our aggression, or because we behave in a culturally offensive manner. People who claim to speak and act in the name of Christ can be as obnoxious as anybody else, even more so when their strident words and ugly attitudes are uttered in a misguided spirit of 'righteous indignation'. In other instances the hostility of the world is simply a case of genuine misunderstanding.

As the Servant of God, Jesus provided the ultimate model of how to relate to the society of which he was a part. He lived close to people, sharing in their social life and everyday activities. He spoke the language of the people, who were amazed at his practical wisdom and spiritual insights. He was in no way remote or 'stand-offish'. On the other hand, he never simply went with the crowd. He was so radically different that his very presence made a significant impact. When John refers to *'the world'* he has in mind the world system that stands in opposition to God and espouses values that are contrary to those of his Kingdom. When these opposing forces laying claim on us discover that we do not belong to them and that we refuse to conform, then they will oppose us at every turn. Elsewhere in the New Testament the servants of Christ are described as *resident aliens* and as *strangers and pilgrims* in this world. Our citizenship and true home lies elsewhere. Servants of Christ have a prior allegiance and a higher calling, as Jesus made clear to his disciples, *'... I have chosen you out of the world. That is why the world hates you'* (15:19). Servants of Christ fulfil a prophetic calling, so we should not be surprised when we suffer a prophet's fate.

Repeatedly, Jesus emphasized his identity with the Father. He taught only what he had received from the Father, and at this point he declared that those who had seen him had seen the Father. Their shared identity could not be closer. Consequently, those who rejected Jesus' claims were without excuse for their sin. Herein lies the difference between the witness of his servants in any age and that of Jesus himself. As forgiven sinners, our witness is of a different order, in that it is marred by our compromise and limited understanding. None of us dare make the same claim as Jesus that *'They hated me without reason'* (15:25).

For first century Jewish believers in Jesus, to be *put out of the synagogue* was a serious punishment, alienating them from friends and family. There would also be serious economic consequences, in that people would refuse to do business with them. As a consequence, the early church in Jerusalem was characterized by poverty and became dependent on gifts from churches in other parts of the Mediterranean world. Suffering is all the more difficult to bear when it comes from those closest to us. But hostility would not stop at social isolation. A number of faithful witnesses would have to face death for their beliefs. In some regions of the world today, those who are bold enough to declare their allegiance to Christ are disowned by their family and face threats upon their life.

As we face difficult times what may seem like an eternity to us in reality is but a *little while* in the planning of God. Endurance is not simply maintaining a regular pace, but being able to work through the difficult times. There will be occasions when we will be tempted to give up. Long-distance runners refer to 'hitting the wall' as they reach that point when they feel that their strength is about to give out. But they know from experience that they have to persevere through that crisis until they get their 'second wind', which will enable them to continue running for many more miles. In many areas of life there are no significant gains without agonizing pain. Some of the most valuable lessons that we learn about ourselves are the most painful.

Have you ever been tempted to give up? What makes you glad you didn't?

During the following forty days the disciples experienced a number of surprising yet brief encounters with the Lord. Then, following Jesus' Ascension into heaven, the Holy Spirit was given so that the nature of their relationship to the Lord Jesus was dramatically changed from that time on. At last they came to appreciate that it was for their good (16:7) that the Lord had gone away, for then they came to know a new level of intimacy with the Lord through his indwelling Spirit. They could address their prayers to the Father directly through Jesus, with the assurance that they will be heard. *'Until now you have not asked for anything in my name. Ask and you will receive, and your joy will be complete'* (John 16:24). Praying in his name meant that their prayers carried his signature. The quality of their prayer life will have a fundamental bearing on their spiritual endurance, as it will with ours.

The disciples claimed that now they understood, when in reality they only understood in part and subsequent events would reveal the limitations of their knowledge. But thankfully, Jesus knew just how little they really knew at that stage, and warned them that they did not believe as much about him as they assumed and professed. The fragility of their faith would be revealed when they eventually abandoned him at his time of trial. Yet, despite everything, they would eventually come together and reach out to turn the world upside down. They would undertake their future mission in joyful response to the Lord's encouragement and claim. *'In this world you will have trouble. But take heart! I have overcome the world'* (16:33).

Counting the cost

The mall is the cathedral now,
its vaulted glass ceilings a testimony
to the old adage that the sky's the limit.

Buy now, pay later is the dayglo creed
posted on every passing window.
Give me credit: I shop, therefore I am.

And down in the food hall,
the kids of the global village
taste and see that the market is good;

a slice of Italy, spices from India,
and America and China come wrapped in
polystyrene for your convenience.

Meanwhile, peacocks strut with their latest handsets
and swap ring-tones beneath the Golden Arches,
in search of textual healing and the capital feeling

that comes with becoming brand new.
Why not slip out of last season's trainers
and into something more *you*?

There seems little more to do
than shop until we drop.
All consuming, and all consumed.

Is there anyone
willing to stand out from this crowd and
Count the cost?

| Taught by the Holy Spirit

John 15:26-27; 16:5-16

... when he, the Spirit of truth, comes, he will guide you into all truth ... he will testify about me. And you also must testify ... (16:13; 15:26, 27)

We are able to endure in the midst of hostility because Jesus has sent the 'Counsellor' to strengthen us and to testify on his behalf. Our strength comes from the combined ministries of Father, Son and Holy Spirit. The Father is the ultimate source, for it is he who sent his Son, who in turn sent the Holy Spirit to indwell and bind together the followers of Christ. Through the Holy Spirit, the one who comes alongside, the mission of Jesus becomes our ministry.

The disciples gathered in the Upper Room had demonstrated their endurance in sticking with Jesus, even when so many others had deserted him along the way. Three times during Jesus' lengthy conversation with his disciples he focused their attention on the ministry of the *'Counsellor'* (*Paraclete*) whom he was about to send. Clearly the role of the Spirit was of central importance at that time. (See *Day Twenty-Six*, where we considered the first of these references to the Spirit.)

No matter how unwilling the disciples were to face the possibility of change, Jesus had to prepare them by bringing repeatedly this unavoidable eventuality to their attention. Although they were not ready to listen on that occasion, in retrospect they would eventually be able to receive his teaching. He assured them, saying, *'It is for your good that I am going away'* (16:7). It was no use their attempting to cling to the past.

Also the Holy Spirit has a wider mission beyond that of indwelling the servants of the Lord. He also works in the hearts of those whom the ascended Lord calls to himself. He convicts the world of its wrongdoing in rejecting the one whom the Father sent, and calls them to change their mind and renounce their sins. He helps people realize that they can never earn their own salvation, for it is only through the crucifixion, resurrection and ascension of the Lord Jesus that they are reconciled to a holy God. They will come to realize that it is not the world that passes judgment on Jesus, but Jesus who passes judgment on the world, and those who reject him.

Jesus knew that there was a limit to the information his apprehensive disciples were able to process at that time. He told them, *'I have much more to say to you, more than you can now bear'* (16:12). Education is not just the off-loading of information. It is giving people at any one time only as much as they are able to take in and process, not only intellectually but emotionally, thereby making it their own. Jesus' teaching methods provide a timeless model. He more often responded to a question with a follow-up question, rather than give a straight answer. He knew that providing ready answers would have robbed people of the thrill of personal discovery. It is that 'ah-ha!' experience of the light dawning that provided the motivation to share what they had learned, thereby reliving the thrill of that moment of realization. The main challenge for the disciples was that this was their last class with him prior to the Cross. He had warned them that he would be with them only a little longer, and, that where he was going they could not go.

Whatever our profession or area of expertise we recognize our need for ongoing education and training. We need to keep abreast of advances in our field and to relate to a changing world culture. So the Lord here reassured his disciples that he was sending to them the *'Spirit of truth, ... [who] will guide you into all truth'* (16:13). He wanted them to realize and acknowledge that they still had a great deal to learn.

During his earthly ministry Jesus acknowledged to his disciples that he did not act independently, but only did what he saw his heavenly Father doing. He declared that the word they heard was not his but came from the Father who sent him. Then Jesus added another link to the communication chain when he told the disciples the Holy Spirit *'... will not speak on his own; he will speak only what he hears, and he will tell you what is yet to come'* (16:13). In the New Testament we are faced with the mystery that in God there is a community of being: Father, Son and Holy Spirit. No one Person of the Trinity operates independently from the other two. They operate with a single purpose in view and activities are intertwined.

Some people might interpret our Lord to mean that the Spirit will bring fresh revelations, adding novel truths to what he has already taught them. But this line of thinking cannot be derived from the text. The Apostle Paul makes clear to the Colossians that in Christ 'are hidden all the treasures of wisdom and knowledge' (2:3). Nothing is to be received as essential for salvation that is not to be found in the New Testament. And if anyone claims divine inspiration for any revelation that contradicts the teachings of Christ, it is to be rejected.

When Jesus spoke of the Holy Spirit leading his disciples into all truth he was referring to the truth that he had already made known to them, but that their grasp of it had been limited. The task of the *Paraclete* was to come alongside them to lead them into a growing comprehension of the depths and heights of the revelation; dimensions as yet unexplored by them. The Gospel of John – the most reflective of the four Gospels – is itself perhaps the most powerful example of this truth in operation. The revealing work of the Holy Spirit is first to reinforce old truths that we have chosen to ignore. Second, he casts new light on old truths in the light of new circumstances. And third, the Spirit reveals things we have overlooked and applies them to new contexts.

> What has the Holy Spirit taught you through your meditation on the scripture passages in 'Way to Serve'?

The ministry of the Holy Spirit is to glorify Jesus and not to detract from him. So we must not be deceived by gurus with their professed spiritual insights arising out of mystical experiences and divine revelations. Recourse to 'higher powers' can prove not only deceptive but also destructive. Throughout John's Gospel, to glorify the Lord is inseparably linked with Jesus' death and resurrection, which events are both the apex of divine revelation and the heart of the gospel.

There are people who privatize the work of the Holy Spirit. They are preoccupied with what they are convinced the Holy Spirit has to say to them personally and individually for the benefit of their own lives or to impose on other people. It can be a brazen form of spiritual blackmail to claim divine authorization for our opinions! When Jesus assured the disciples that the Spirit of Truth will be given to *you*, the second person pronoun used is plural and not singular. The Spirit is given to the community – it is not the private possession of any individual, not even the prophet.

Therefore, we need to check our understanding of spiritual truth against the core doctrine of the church maintained throughout the centuries. Also, we need to be accountable to one another by providing spiritual discernment and correction. The truth imparted by the Spirit does not consist of encyclopaedic knowledge but the heart of the gospel in relation to the people of God and their place in world history. Neither does it give believers a monopoly on truth or provide a 'hotline' to heaven. While here on earth we only know in part and we see dimly through a fuzzy mirror (1 Cor. 13:12).

Servants of the Lord in every age are utterly reliant on the indwelling of the Holy Spirit to guide them as to what their Master requires of them. He also gives us the appropriate gifts in order to operate effectively, as well as the fruit of Christ-like character to ensure that we are authentic and trustworthy witnesses.

Clarity

Moments of clarity
fall rarely upon me.
There are times
when I strain my eyes
to see how it all
should be, and a shape
blurs into focus.
A sense that Someone
is letting me in on a
divine secret.

More often
I find myself longing
for presence but
sensing absence,
as if the responsibility rests
with me and me alone.

But then, the wind gusts
and the trees bend and sway,
and I recall
that the invisible God sent Someone
to cajole and whisper
and dance and brush against our cheek,
to breathe life through us
and lead us onwards.

And for a moment, again,
things becomes clear,
and it feels like
life could be a breeze.

Sent into a hostile world

John 17:1–26

As you sent me into the world, I have sent them into the world (18)

Jesus concluded his ministry among his disciples with a prayer. Beginning with a prayer for himself, it moved on to express his concern for his disciples and extended from them to future disciples who would become servants of God through their witness. It is the longest and most extensive prayer in the four Gospels. The fact that it was uttered in the presence of his disciples indicated Jesus' intention to be overheard and leave a lasting impression with them.

Jesus spoke to his heavenly Father as though his mission was already accomplished. It is not simply that it was almost over, but that he saw with the eye of faith beyond the dreadful events that were about to take place. His prayer was uttered from the perspective of eternity and it was to be his ongoing prayer from heaven as he continues to this day to intercede before his heavenly Father as our great High Priest.

The sequence of the prayer is significant. Jesus earthly ministry brought the kingdom into the world by giving eternal life to all who came to Christ in repentance and faith. Those who came to him out of the world are then sent back into the world. Mission contributed to the growth of the Kingdom as his servants went into the world to witness to all that God in Christ had done for them and among them. They would reach out to their contemporaries who would in turn reach future generations to bring into being the Church of Jesus Christ in all the world in anticipation of the return of Christ. The sequence of events is, first, the Kingdom that comes as the gift of God, then, mission as the servants of the King move out into the world, leading to the formation of the Church as generations of new believers gather together in Christ's name.

The supreme goal of Jesus' life and ministry was to bring glory to God. His servants in every age share that same objective. John began by informing us that Jesus knew that *'the time* [literally hour] *has come'* (1), a moment that would change the course of history. He was about to return to his heavenly Father with his mission on earth accomplished. What was the central purpose of that mission? It was to give eternal life to all whom the Father gave to Jesus. His entire life work had been to give glory to the Father and not to seek it for himself. The role of servants is always to serve and in so doing focus attention on the master. They never seek the limelight for themselves.

Jesus was able to say that *he had completed the work* (3) that God had given him to do. Faithful servants are those who finish well. God is not glorified by half-finished or abandoned projects. Our enthusiasm must be matched by our lifetime commitment. With his mission now accomplished Jesus was about to return to the glory in heaven that he had temporarily laid aside. Restored to his position at his Father's right hand he was then given authority over all peoples. It is this authority that forms the basis of the Great Commission that he entrusted to his disciples after his resurrection, sending them to all peoples everywhere with the invitation to join them in following Christ.

Jesus turned next to his disciples in his prayer. During the three years, they had had ample opportunity to observe him at close quarters. They had seen his compassion for the crowds as well as for needy individuals, and Jesus always had time for one-on-one ministry. They had observed him under extreme pressure with the demands of the crowds and the hostility of the religious authorities. At all times they had seen the Father faithfully and flawlessly represented through his life, words and ministry. Every servant carries the responsibility of representing and guarding the reputation of the master by the manner in which they serve.

Jesus did not claim the disciples as his own but gave them back to the Father. Servants are not characterized by possessiveness but in giving everything to their master. Yet again Jesus confessed his absolute dependence on his Father. Throughout his earthly ministry he had served as the channel and not the source, drawing on the presence and power of the Holy Spirit in his life.

True disciples are those individuals who have received Jesus' teaching as coming from the Father and who know in personal experience that his teaching has had a transformative impact on their lives. Notice that the heart of Jesus' teaching does not consist in moral exhortations but in coming to terms with who he is. His words has supreme authority and his disciples *'accepted them'* (8), i.e. they believed them and proved them to be true in their own experience. This does not imply that they had 'arrived' spiritually, but rather that they were on target and making progress.

Faith-based obedience is an essential pre-requisite for service. Jesus was fully aware that his servants faced great challenges and dangers. So, in their hearing, he prayed for their protection as they embarked on their future ministry. There could be no greater encouragement and joy than for them to know that Jesus was their continuing intercessor. They had known Jesus' protection on many an occasion during the past three years, and now Jesus handed over that responsibility to his Father.

This is the only place in the New Testament where the form of address *Holy Father* (11) is used. It is God's holiness that will protect them and keep them united in the presence of a hostile world. Once again Jesus returned to the theme of joy that is completed in him. As such it is not dependent on outward circumstance. Rather it is a defiant and resilient joy that the world cannot take away, because in Christ we have overcome the world.

The word of God that had taken root in the disciples' lives set them apart and made them different, which is the root meaning of *sanctify*. But they were not set apart to be isolated from the world, still less to be rescued from it. They had been set apart in order to be sent back into the world. There was a direct continuity between the ministry of Jesus and that of his disciples. They were sent under the same authority, with the same purpose and in the same

Are you prepared to be set apart in order to be sent back into the world?

power as Jesus. Their mission was not survival but service. They were to become immersed in the world without being overwhelmed by it.

The last part of Jesus' prayer consisted of his intercession on behalf of those who would come to believe through the witness of his disciples. Despite their glaring limitations Jesus had complete confidence in them. It was the witness of his apostles that provided the foundation for the belief of all subsequent generations as they spoke and wrote under the inspiration of the Holy Spirit, providing a reliable record of his words and actions. The overriding concern of Jesus at this point was for the ongoing mission of his servants to bring into being a new humanity, as diverse and antagonistic people were made one by the reconciling message of the Gospel that unites us with God and with one another. Our oneness consists of our new identity as adopted sons and daughters called to serve God, serve each other and serve the world for which Jesus gave his life. Jesus' continuing expression of concern for unity among his servants arose out of the ongoing squabbling and jockeying among them, which distressed him greatly.

The prospect of every disciple becoming a witness opened up the possibility of exponential growth from generation to generation. We see something of this potential fulfilled with the rapid expansion of the early church during the first three centuries. From a small and geographically restricted primary group it became a movement that spread rapidly throughout the Roman Empire and then beyond its borders. In our own day we are also seeing rapid expansion of the Christian church not in the West but in the East and southern hemisphere: in many areas of Africa south of the Sahara, Latin America and parts of Asia.

God is glorified through the spread of the gospel not only in the numerical growth of the Church but also in transformed lives. This transformation does not come about simply through moral exhortation, but through the communion that the believer is privileged to share with the Father and the Son. Such is the astounding request that Jesus made on our behalf: '... *that all of them may be one, Father, just as you are in me and I am in you. May they also be in us so that the world may believe that you have sent me*' (John 17:21). Writing to the church in Corinth, the apostle Paul explained how the glory of Jesus came to be reflected in their lives (2 Cor. 3:18), the glory, which we glimpse dimly now, in which we will bask for eternity in heaven. This is the 'made in Heaven' trademark of an authentic servant.

Jesus' prayer concluded with a solemn pledge to his Father. Here Jesus reassured his disciples that he would continue to make himself known to them, not only by the knowledge that he would continue to impart, but also by the love that he would be pouring into their lives. After this there was nothing more to be said. He went out with his disciples to face betrayal, desertion, trial, scourging and crucifixion.

Brand loyalty

We like to wear our hearts on our sleeve,
and a logo on our chest;
striving to be set apart as individuals in an age of conformity.
The advertisers tell us to 'Just do it',
and for a moment we feel alive and forget that
everyone else is just doing it too.

Paul once wrote of being branded –
before the days of Adidas and Nike and Vodaphone.
He said that he had taken the marks of Christ
literally, bearing the scars
to show that he would not conform
to the pattern of this world any longer.

Branded as a follower of Christ,
not by his fish badge or bumper sticker,
not by the God channel he watched
or the on-line version of the Bible he subscribed to,
and not by a sub-cultural affiliation to a flock of sheep,
but by treading a narrower path; by making a difference.

That's brand loyalty for you.

way to
serve

part 6

Servant communities

The people of God impacting
the world

day 31 | Serving boldly

Acts 4:1–31

Now, Lord, consider their threats and enable your servants to speak your word with great boldness (29)

'Servant' is a bad word for those who equate it with servitude. But for the servant of God – as we have emphasized in a number of places – the idea of service carries a different meaning. Rather than suggesting demeaning relationships, it is a title of honour, signifying that we are primarily accountable to Jesus Christ as Lord of our lives and before whom we submit in humility. It is a service that is truly liberating, for we are freed from thinking that we are simply to submit to other people's agendas and control. Those ministering in Jesus' name, which means working under his authority and in accordance with his will, are not easily intimidated. Peter and John provide impressive examples of boldness when called to account by the Jewish authorities in Jerusalem.

Peter had demonstrated extraordinary courage in preaching to the crowds on the day of Pentecost under the watchful eyes of the temple authorities. There had been no time for him to prepare his message on that occasion – he had simply seized his chance. When a second opportunity presented itself Peter once again rose to the occasion.

The authorities responsible for law and order in the temple were understandably concerned at the public interest aroused both by the healing of the crippled man and the message preached by Peter. The Jerusalem authorities felt the pressure to take urgent action to stop this movement in its tracks. It was growing too rapidly to be ignored.

The authorities threw into prison both Peter, the spokesperson, and John, his silent partner, to cool their heals for the night. The next morning they are brought before Annas the former high priest and his son-in-law Caiaphas, who currently held the office, as well as other leading officials. The authorities hoped that a night in prison, coupled with their hostile questioning and a stern warning, might bring sufficient pressure to cause them to quiet down and disperse.

Their leaders might thereby be persuaded to return to their homes in Galilee. Furthermore, if these followers of Jesus subsequently broke the court order by refusing to remain silent they could then be rearrested on the more serious charge of contempt of court.

But they showed no indication of being overawed by the occasion. When they were asked an opening direct question, *'By what power or what name did you do this?'* (7) they gave a clear answer, *'. . . by the name of Jesus Christ of Nazareth'* (10). They did not beat about the bush. And neither should we.

After denying his Lord by the campfire in the temple courtyard, not far from where he now stood, Peter had learned his lesson. But on this occasion he stood before his examiners filled with the power of the Holy Spirit (8). Confidence and boldness continued to be character traits of the early Christians as is recorded on six subsequent occasions in Acts (9:27f.; 13:46; 14:3; 18:26; 19:6; 26:26) and two references in Paul's letters (Eph. 6:20; 1 Thess. 2:2).

> Are you seeking to be filled with the Holy Spirit every day?

The strength of their evidence also enhanced the boldness of their witness. They were not trained theologians, so they confined their testimony to what they knew. They were unshakeable in their conviction that Jesus was the Son of God and the Messiah sent to deliver God's people. They had healed a crippled man in the name of Jesus, whom they charged their examining authorities with having put to death, but whom God had raised to life. The very one they rejected was the key figure on whom they all depended according to God's plans laid long ago (11). *'Salvation is found in no one else'* (12). In rejecting Jesus they had left themselves with no alternative, for God had no 'plan B'. At this point in his account of the incident, Luke hinted that it was the authorities who were in fact on trial, rather than the disciples! The Jewish rulers found themselves having to make a tough decision. The crippled man was standing before them as incontrovertible evidence. Presumably many, if not all of them, would have seen him often as they entered and left the temple. They could not deny that a miracle had taken place.

Peter and John continued to show their boldness by their rejection of the court order to remain silent. They do this on the grounds that they were answerable to a higher court. In so doing they turned the issue back on to their accusers (19). Immediately following their release Peter and John went back to their own people to report what had happened to them. The whole group now prayed together that they would all be given continuing boldness to maintain their witness in the face of opposition from the authorities. They also prayed that the Lord would continue to confirm their witness with signs and wonders. In response to their prayers they experienced a powerful reassurance of God's presence with them, shaking the building where they are meeting, and received a fresh filling of the Holy Spirit, enabling them to speak the word of God with boldness (see Acts 1:8). Here is a further reminder that believers in the twenty-first century, as well as the first century, need the power of the Holy Spirit to be effective in our testimony and that might entail a shake-up!

Life Line

When do you think I should draw the line?
When someone fails to appreciate my fine words?
When those who follow me start grumbling?
When people start taking me for granted?
When I feel like they're talking behind my back?
When my friends lose their bottle?
When someone I've trusted betrays me?
When things look like they might get out of hand?
When it's actually getting dangerous?
When there's still time to pull out?
When everything I've ever stood for is thrown back in my face?
When it gets physical?
When my life is on the line?

My God, my God,
How on earth did you stand back and do nothing?

Sharing resources

Acts 4:32 – 5:11

There were no needy persons among them. For from time to time those who owned lands or houses sold them, brought the money from the sales and put it at the apostles' feet, and it was distributed to anyone as he had need (Acts 4:34, 35)

When times are hard the community must pull together in order for the members to survive. We who are twenty-first century Western Christians are shaped by a culture that emphasizes personal rights and individual resourcefulness, rather than corporate responsibility, accountability and mutual dependence. This incident reminds us that the church in Jerusalem was birthed in poverty and in a climate of growing hostility displayed by the people who exercised political, religious and economic power. This is also the case today for believers in many areas of the world. We need to consider the mutual support that the church displayed in a context that demanded the pooling of resources as a survival strategy.

From day one the church in Jerusalem displayed its inner strength by the mutual commitment demonstrated by its members. Following the outpouring of the Holy Spirit on the day of Pentecost that brought about the first great ingathering of new believers, they *'were together and had everything in common. Selling their possessions and goods, they gave to anyone as he had need'* (2:44, 45). Common ownership was not a *requirement* for membership of the community of believers – it becomes clear in today's story that contributing to the common purse was a voluntary action, and, rather than routinely, the action here described occurred *'from time to time'* (4:34). It also appears that the community extended its generosity beyond its own impoverished members, for it *'enjoyed the favour of all the people'* (2:47). The rapid growth of the church meant that social problems also became a major concern. By the time that the incident described in today's reading occurred, there were already an estimated five thousand men (4:4), to which total we must add an unknown number of women and children. This provides the wider context against which we must consider the inspiring story of Barnabas, followed by the tragic account of Ananias and Sapphira.

The early church was characterized by a unity of heart and purpose that was put to the test as it continued to grow in numbers. Would it be able to retain and reinforce its shared values, or would its increase in size result in a lessening of commitment? This issue had to be addressed at the outset. In order for the church to retain its values and spiritual vibrancy it had to continue to experience the outpouring of the Holy Spirit (4:31). It could not simply rely on human resources. The dynamic provided by the Holy Spirit was evidenced both by powerful proclamation of the good news of Jesus Christ and in a continuing expression of love in practical ways. At the same time that the apostles continued to *testify to the resurrection* (33) in defiance of the court order, those who possessed property were prepared to sell up to contribute to a common purse to help out the poorest of their members so that *there were no needy persons among them* (34). Proclamation in the power of the Holy Spirit is filled with grace that draws people to Christ rather than driving them away.

As people continued to transfer their assets, so the administrative burden on the apostles increased until it reached the point where they were in danger of being diverted from their spiritual responsibilities and eventually overwhelmed in trying to respond to the growing financial and social needs (6:1–7). Among those making a significant contribution was Barnabas, who is singled out as a positive example. He is evidently a person who, in addition to having a 'deep pocket', had a big heart. His ministry of generosity was

How genuine is your generosity?

matched by his ministry of encouragement, signified by his name change from Joseph to Barnabas (4:36). He is later described by Luke as *a good man, full of the Holy Spirit and faith* (11:24) and was to continue to play a significant role in the life of the early church (9:27; 11:22–27; 15:35). Unlike Barnabas, some benefactors are prepared to write fat cheques but are not so willing to get personally involved.

If Barnabas is presented as a positive example of generosity, the story of the married couple Ananias and Sapphira is recorded as a strong warning against duplicity. This is a shocking incident that raises many unanswered questions because Luke does not provide adequate information. The couple decided on a plan intended to deceive the leadership of the Jerusalem church. *'With his wife's full knowledge he [Ananias] kept back part of the money for himself, but brought the rest and put it at the apostles' feet'* (5:2). The reader is not informed as to their motive. Was their deception designed to gain influence in the new movement? There are many examples of church members attempting to buy their way into positions of influence, for the person who pays the piper calls the tune. If their deception had been allowed to go undetected and unpunished it would have jeopardized the future of the movement. When the Holy Spirit is outpoured in blessing, he may also act in severe judgment. Both Ananias and Sapphira lied not only to the apostles but also to the Holy Spirit (5:3, 9). Ananias took the action he did because, as Peter made plain to him, *'Satan has so filled your heart'* (5:3). Both Ananias and Sapphira pay with their lives with what appears to be heart attacks brought on by the shock of their exposure. But their sudden death is a divine punishment not simply a human consequence.

The impact on the Christian community is one of shock and awe (5:11). The lessons for us in terms of our own giving are clear. We need to be generous towards to the needy, beginning with the community of believers, whether our own congregation or impoverished and suffering believers in other parts of the world. Also we need to be honest about our motives. Our giving is always for the benefit of others and never to enhance our own position.

Shock and awe

Drop dead! I don't believe
that a loving God would,
for one moment, pull a stunt
like that. Well, not the kind
of God I'd like to believe in,
mister. Anyway, this is the
age of the consumer, and the
consumer is king.

I don't
buy that stuff about
paying the ultimate price
for anything.

Who would?

One thing leads to another

Acts 6:1-8; 8:1-8

... choose seven men from among you who are known to be full of the Spirit and wisdom (6:3)

In order to sustain healthy growth in a church every member must be involved in some form of Christian service. Smaller churches tend to have a higher percentage of their members involved. But the larger the church becomes, the easier it is for an increasing percentage of those who attend to remain inactive, or for previously active persons to retire to the sidelines.

The dominant model we find today is of a church in which the twenty percent serve and entertain the eighty percent. This is far short of the ideal in which every member of the body of Christ contributes some form of service according to their gifts, calling and passion. Furthermore, when churches are experiencing an impressive net growth, it is all too easy to overlook those whose needs are not being met. This was the situation that the church in Jerusalem was beginning to face.

The first five chapters of the book of Acts record the impressive numerical growth resulting from the outreach ministries of the apostles within Jerusalem and in the surrounding Judean towns. Most of the resulting increase in believers occurred among the Judean Aramaic speaking Jews who were native to the area. But the needs brought into the fellowship by that stream of new people made increasing ministry demands – and the apostles were in danger of being overwhelmed with the challenge of consolidating their gains. Being so preoccupied with communicating the Good News, they had neither the time nor energy to address a growing problem that had arisen in one section of the Jerusalem church.

The pressing need was among believers in Jerusalem, Greek-speaking Jews from around the Mediterranean world who had settled in the Holy City to spend their remaining years there. The most vulnerable within their community were the widows, who no longer had the financial and emotional support of their spouse or extended family. Consequently, they became dependent on the generosity of the church to relieve their poverty and provide meals on a daily basis. As this need was largely confined to one segment of the church it was not seen as a priority by the Aramaic-speakers, who held the purse strings. Any needy Aramaic speakers were benefiting from the benevolence funds that had been established by their community and it was these funds that were being dispersed unfairly.

Once the apostles became aware of the extent and urgency of the need they took prompt measures to deal with the situation. They explained to the church that that they must not be diverted from their primary mission as apostles, called to evangelize, gather new converts into communities of believers, and to teach them and to pray for them. Other individuals would need to shoulder the responsibility. This highlights an important lesson for servants, namely that we are not called to respond personally to every need that comes our way. The task of church leaders is to ensure that genuine and urgent needs are met through the involvement of other workers.

The apostles invited all of the disciples in the Jerusalem church to come up with seven names from among their number. Wisely, in order to avoid any accusation of bias, the apostles did not themselves make the selection; instead, they established the criteria for the selection: practical people who were also trustworthy, fair and wise, *'full of the Spirit and wisdom'* (6:3) – trustworthy, as they would be held responsible for handling the funds, and good organizers, to ensure that they identified the needy widows and provided a reliable meals programme.

It is significant that all of the seven people selected had Greek names. Although it was not uncommon for Hebrew-speaking Jews to take Greek names, it can be no accident that all seven met the qualification. The individuals chosen had to be highly respected by the community they served and preferably one of their own.

These seven were called 'deacons' or servants. On the surface it might seem a mundane form of ministry, yet each was appointed personally to their task by the apostles with prayer and the laying on of hands. Servants should never be taken for granted or the significance of their contribution downplayed. Furthermore, it became evident that there was more going on behind the scenes than appeared on the surface. Their appointment led to a further growth spurt.

At this time the ranks of the new disciples swelled further with the addition of a great number of priests who became obedient to the faith (6:7). New Testament scholars estimated that around eight thousand priests served the temple on a rotational basis. They would have had ample opportunity to hear the witness of the apostles and other disciples who continued to meet regularly in the Temple courtyard and to attend the daily services. They would also have witnessed people being healed and delivered from the power of evil spirits. The conversion of significant numbers of the Temple priests must have focused even greater attention on the Aramaic-speaking section of the church.

The deacons were soon engaged in a wider ministry than the arranging of distribution of food. This was especially true in the case of Stephen and Philip. Stephen was described as *'a man full of God's grace and power, [who] did great wonders and miraculous signs among the people'* (6:8). Before long his work among the Greek-speaking segment of the population came to the attention of the members of the Synagogue of the Freedmen comprising Greek-speaking Jews from North Africa and modern south-east Turkey who had been freed from slavery. They quickly came to regard Stephen as a special threat to their community. They decided that he had to be stopped so that no more of their number would be attracted to those who followed the Way of Jesus. When their attempts to out-argue him failed, they persuaded some men to charge him with blasphemy and of speaking against the Temple and the Law of Moses. These accusations were brought before the supreme Jewish court, the Sanhedrin, who found Stephen guilty and punished him by stoning him to death – the first Christian martyr.

His death unleashed a persecution directed against the more

vulnerable Greek-speaking section of the church, which had migrated to Jerusalem from outside the country. The apostles, as leaders of the Aramaic-speakers were not targeted, for the time being at least. By going after the Greek-speakers first, the Jewish authorities put the Aramaic-speaking believers on notice that they would be next if they did not abandon their foolish notions and return to the orthodox Jewish faith.

The Greek-speaking believers were forced to flee Jerusalem, scattering throughout Judea and Samaria. Among them was Philip, another of the seven deacons. If the Jerusalem authorities had hoped to intimidate these believers into silence, they were badly mistaken, for Philip immediately began spreading the Good News of Jesus throughout the towns of Samaria with considerable success. Philip, who began by serving at tables, became a notable evangelist.

The Holy Spirit next led Philip to a location on the desert road from Jerusalem to Egypt in order to meet up with an Ethiopian official. As the official rode along in his chariot, Philip heard him reading aloud from a scroll of Isaiah. Philip approached the official, offering to interpret the Scriptures. His explanation resulted in the Ethiopian coming to believe in Jesus as Messiah.

Having baptized him, Philip returned to Samaria and then settled in the Roman administrative centre of Caesarea, where he continued his evangelistic ministry. Over twenty years later he was still there, for the apostle Paul stayed with him on returning from his third missionary journey. Luke in his Acts account refers to him as *'Philip the evangelist'*, the only person identified by name as an evangelist in the New Testament. And Luke also added that he had four unmarried daughters who prophesied (21:8, 9), referring to another form of service that was prevalent in the early church. For both Stephen and Philip, one thing led to another.

We can learn from the apostles' action the need to focus on what God has called us to do, resisting pressures to become sidetracked. From Stephen and Philip we learn not to remain limited in what we think we can do, but to be open to the possibility that God may want to give us new gifts in order to redirect or expand our service.

When we embark on a life of service to Christ, no matter how humble or mundane our work might appear, it is significant both in the eyes of God and as a contribution to the entire ministry of Christ to his people – and through his people to the wider world. When we prove ourselves faithful in the first task, then the Lord might well entrust us with wider responsibilities and give fresh gifts for ministry.

One thing leads to another
Consider a yawn:
a big, fat, slow yawn.
Are you yawning yet?
One thing leads to another.
And if you're in public,
it's possible the yawn is spreading.

One thing leads to another:
a word, spoken into sadness,
or a kind extravagance
that lightens a heavy day.

If a butterfly flaps its wings in Tokyo,
it can create something of a storm in Texas.

You may just be a bright spark,
but kindle the flame and good news
can spread like wild fire.

One thing leads to another,
but are you ready for where
this might go? Running the
bookstall, running the youth group,
running the church, running the race ...

And yet, Someone took the lead
a long time ago and ran things very differently.
So that we might run straight into the
arms of love.

day 34 | Coaching the next generation of leaders

Acts 15:36 – 16:5

The brothers ... spoke well of him [Timothy]. Paul wanted to take him along on the journey (16:2, 3)

In our service for Christ do we habitually work alone or alongside other people? Paul made it his practice to travel with a team in each of the three missionary journeys recorded in Acts. The members consisted of mature individuals such as Barnabas and Silas, who were senior representatives of the church in Jerusalem, as well as juniors like John Mark and Timothy. Leaders must always have an eye to the future, establishing and expanding the base of leadership in order that the next generation of leaders is in place when the time comes for them to step down or they are no longer around.

How many of us can look back to a time when a mature Christian took us under his or her wing, investing time in us so that we could learn from their example? Young believers need to be encouraged by being invited to tag along and learn by observation until the time that we can be entrusted with tasks to do on our own while working under supervision. We also grow in stature as Christian leaders show such confidence in us.

Is there someone whom you should be coaching and mentoring?

Leaders who have a deep concern for the urgent proclamation of the gospel can sometimes clash over the best means of pursuing that goal. On this occasion a sharp difference of opinion arose between Paul and Barnabas over whether they would take John Mark along with them on their second journey, which began as a follow-up visit to the churches of Galatia. Mindful of the rough treatment that Paul and his companions had received on their first visit, he foresaw the distinct possibility that Mark would insist on returning home, as he had on their first journey.

Paul is understandably convinced that it will prove too much for Mark. Another reason for the disagreement between Paul and Barnabas concerned the latter's refusal to eat with Gentiles, which would cause an awkward situation among the predominantly Gentile churches in Galatia.

Barnabas, on the other hand, was prepared to give Mark a second chance. The two leaders resolved their differences by going their separate ways. While Paul headed back to Galatia, Barnabas and Mark returned to Cyprus, which had been the first port of call on their first journey. By splitting into two teams they could cover the ground more quickly. It is also likely that Barnabas would prove to be a more suitable coach than Paul in the case of John Mark. At this stage Paul did not have a very high opinion of him, whereas Barnabas saw his future potential and was prepared to invest time in him. He had the reputation of being an encourager, and in addition he had family ties to Mark (Col. 4:10). Their decision proved to be a wise one, for Mark evidently did well and blossomed under Barnabas' care. Years later, Paul came to recognize Mark as a valued colleague and asks Timothy to send Mark to minister to him during his second imprisonment in Rome (2 Tim. 4:11).

Paul embarked on his second missionary journey, accompanied by Silas, travelling west by way of a pass through the mountains known as the Cilician Gates. This brought them to Lystra, which was the furthest point in Paul's first journey. It is there that Paul renews contact with the young convert Timothy, whom he had brought to faith in Christ, along with his mother Eunice and grandmother Lois (1 Cor. 4:17; 2 Tim. 1:5). Just as Barnabas' investment in the life of Mark proved fruitful in the long term, so did Paul's coaching of the young Timothy, who began his wider ministry in his home territory of Galatia.

Timothy was from a mixed home. On his mother's side of the family they were Jews, whereas his father was a Greek and not a believer. Although according to Jewish custom Timothy should have been circumcised, for some reason the ceremony had not been performed. Whether this was due to the opposition of his father or the fact that his mother, although personally devout, was not allowed to practise her faith publicly, we do not know. Mark's mixed parentage meant that he was able to relate to both the Jewish and Gentile communities. He had already earned a good reputation among the believers not only in his hometown but also in Iconium, 18 miles away. In order to ensure his acceptance among Jewish believers and to minister in the wider Jewish community Paul had Timothy circumcised. This would save him being referred to as 'illegitimate', a disparaging tag applied to uncircumcised Jews of mixed marriages.

We know more about Timothy's future ministry than the brief references to John Mark. Timothy was commissioned for his missionary work through the laying on of hands of Paul and the elders (1 Tim. 1:18; 4:14). Paul sent him as his special representative to encourage the new believers in Thessalonica and as Paul's representative to Corinth. He accompanied Paul on his visit to Jerusalem to deliver the collection from the churches to relieve the impoverished Jerusalem Christians. He was later left in charge in Ephesus. Despite his poor health and timid disposition, Paul provided him with encouragement and places his confidence in him. Perhaps, he had learned his lesson over his harsh treatment of Mark, causing him to modify his attitude and make greater allowances for youthful immaturity!

The examples of Mark and Timothy underline the importance of identifying and providing coaching for young potential leaders. This is as important in our day as in theirs, especially as many congregations today have an average age considerably older than the communities that surround them. In order to have younger congregations we need many more younger leaders.

Growing up

Young man, you're not really old enough
to assume too much responsibility;
your words seem a little impertinent,
a tad brusque. There's a bit of growing up
to do before you mature into the real deal.

That stuff about the bread of life
and the good shepherd and lost coins ...
it's all very well, but I think you need to
learn how to explain yourself a bit better.

You're leaving yourself far too open
to interpretation; you'll soon learn to
leave them in absolutely no doubt.
In the meantime, why not work with the
children or the youth and let us get on
with the important stuff?

Serving anytime, anywhere

Acts 18:1-28

[In Corinth Paul] met a Jew named Aquila, a native of Pontus, who had recently come from Italy with his wife Priscilla ... he stayed and worked with them ... (1-3) ... [When Paul] sailed for Syria [he was] accompanied by Priscilla and Aquila (18)

Priscilla and Aquila were a remarkable couple. As servants of God they were prepared to go anywhere anytime. Wherever they lived their home became a meeting place as churches became established in their city. We must remember that there were no purpose-built church buildings until the close of the second century, so, for about 150 years the believers mostly met in private homes. The mobility of Priscilla and Aquila indicates the relative ease of travel in the first century Roman world, with good Roman built roads safeguarded by the Roman peace. That mobility was not to be matched around the Mediterranean world until the close of the Middle Ages.

Aquila was a Jew who was born and grew up in Pontus, a region bordering on the Black Sea (modern north-western Turkey). From there, at some point in his life, he had moved to Rome. We know nothing of the background of his wife Priscilla (Prisca was the shortened form of her name) whom he may have met in Rome. When Paul met the couple during his first visit to Corinth it appears that they were already Christians. They had probably been converted in Rome through the Jewish followers of Christ in that city, some of whom may have been in Jerusalem for the Feast of Pentecost following the crucifixion of Christ. There they had heard the preaching of the apostle Peter that had led to their repentance, faith and baptism, before returning home from their pilgrimage.

In about AD 49, the Emperor Claudius' pronounced an edict that expelled all Jews from Rome. The Roman historian Suetonius informs us that this was in response to disturbances among the Jews over someone named Chrestus, which was a common misspelling of 'Christ'. Priscilla and Aquila fled from Rome to Corinth, where they were already located when Paul arrived. These servants were guided by God to be in the right place at the right time. Sometimes in our own lives disruptive events may occur that are part of the larger purposes of God of which we are completely unaware, as we have seen before in the lives of a number of God's servants, such as Abraham and Joseph.

The couple worked together in their ministry of hospitality, teaching and encouragement. It is intriguing that Paul referred to them as 'Priscilla and Aquila', mentioning the wife before her husband, going against the social conventions of the time. Some commentators have conjectured that this was possibly because Priscilla was of a higher social standing than her husband. However, it is more likely that it points to the fact that she played a more prominent role in their team ministry.

The apostle Paul made it his practice to work with a team, but arrived alone in Corinth, where he was in need of friends. Priscilla and Aquila made contact with him, possibly at the synagogue. They offered him not only hospitality, but also the opportunity to make a livelihood – both Aquila and Paul shared the same trade as tent-makers. Tents were made either from goats' hair or from leather and Aquila and Paul may have made a variety of leather goods. Paul continued to support himself by this means until Silas and Timothy arrived from Macedonia with financial support provided by the believers in the cities Paul had previously visited.

Paul also needed the emotional support of Priscilla and Aquila. He was particularly nervous as he faced the challenges presented by a city notorious for its loose living. In addition, he contemplated the likelihood of reprisals from the Jews following the rejection of his message by the majority of the members of the synagogue. Their anger had been further inflamed by the conversion of Crispus, the synagogue ruler. And to further aggravate matters, Paul had set up next door to the synagogue in the house of Titius Justus, an uncircumcised Gentile worshiper in the synagogue.

This was one of the few places where the ascended Lord is quoted as speaking directly to one of his servants, comforting Paul (9, 10). By that time he had already met up with two of the Lord's servants, and had seen the response of Crispus and his entire household as well as many other Corinthians who had believed and been baptized. The Lord assured him that these were just the first fruits of a much larger spiritual harvest.

No doubt Priscilla and Aquila shared Paul's apprehension in the aftermath of their own experience in Rome. But they remained loyal, endangering their lives for his sake and the gospel's. True friends continue their support no matter how rough the going becomes. With Paul they faced the angry mob hired by the Jews. These trouble-makers even turned on Sosthenes, Crispus' replacement as ruler of the synagogue. Had he too become a follower of Christ by this time, or at least admitted that he was sympathetic to the message?

After spending some considerable time in Corinth, Paul decided to head back to Syria and his base church in Antioch. Priscilla and Aquila accompanied him as far as Ephesus, where Paul, as was his custom, visited the synagogue to argue his case that Jesus was the Messiah. Declining the invitation of the members to spend more time with them, he left his friends to bear their witness to Christ while he continued with his journey, promising to return as soon as he was able.

Paul had evidently taught them well because Priscilla and Aquila had a significant ministry during Paul's absence. A Jew named Apollos arrived at Ephesus from the North African port of Alexandria, where the church was already in existence. Alexandria was noted for its speculative theology and boasted one of the greatest libraries in the ancient world. The city also had a very large Jewish community. During his time there Apollos had acquired a deep and comprehensive knowledge of the Scriptures. He had also been instructed in *'the way of the Lord'* (25), which presumably included information on how Jesus had fulfilled the Old Testament prophecies relating to the long-expected Messiah, and about the life, ministry and teaching of Jesus. But there was a serious limitation, in that

Apollos only knew about the baptism of John, whose baptism of repentance was to prepare Israel spiritually for the coming of God's kingdom amongst them. It is not clear whether Apollos had already received the Holy Spirit by the time he arrived in Ephesus, or whether Luke was referring to his fervour of spirit. In any case, he needed to be baptized into the name of Christ and to know the fullness of the Spirit's presence in his life.

Once again, we see a specific example of Priscilla and Aquila offering hospitality. They not only befriended Apollos by inviting him to their home but they also explained to him the way of God more adequately (26). As learned and eloquent as was Apollos, he was open to receive further instruction from this devoted couple. Furthermore, they along with all the other believers in their fellowship encouraged Apollos in his desire to go to Corinth and continue his ministry there, especially now that he had a better grasp of the essentials of the faith. They wrote him a letter of introduction, which indicated their confidence in him as a debater with the Jews and as a teacher of those enquiring about the faith. They knew from personal experience what a tough challenge he would face there. Evidently, their confidence in him was not misplaced (27, 28).

Priscilla and Aquila are mentioned three more times in the New Testament. They were still in Ephesus three years later when Paul wrote his first letter to the Corinthians from there. Two years latter they were back in Rome and Paul sends his greetings to them and to the church meeting in their home. But still their travels were not over, for when Paul wrote to Timothy in Ephesus around AD 62, he sent his greetings to them there. Notice that they travelled between the three strategic centres of Rome, Corinth and Ephesus. In each place they encountered great challenges in the form of pagan religion, as well as the hostility of their fellow Jews. But wherever they were, their home became a magnet for the believing community and a centre of hospitality, teaching and encouragement.

If the church is to continue to expand in our day it will be through the grass-roots initiatives of people like Priscilla and Aquila rather than through top-down planning and big budget campaigns and building projects. Encouragingly, there are increasing numbers of people who are prepared to open their homes and share the Good News of Christ. People are more likely to be attracted to Christ as they are welcomed into such company – where they have the opportunity to see the gospel in action through the lives of those who profess Christ, serve their communities and offer friendship with no 'strings attached'. Priscilla and Aquila were dedicated servants of God, who moved not in order to go up in the world but to get out into the world to make a difference. May we serve with that same clarity of vision and sacrificial commitment.

Open

I'd like to think I'm open
to new ideas,
fresh possibilities,
a touch of bohemia
to brighten the 9 to 5;
I'd like to think I'm open
minded, open
to persuasion, open
enough to listen
without prejudice.

I'd like to think I'm open
to those who need help,
to people who are different,
even those who smell poor
and look shabby;
in fact, I'd like to think I'm open
24 hours a day to the call of God.

But I've found that being open
is much harder
than I'd like to think.

way to serve

part 7

Letters to churches on active service

Cultivate the mind of Christ

Philippians 2:1–11

Each of you should look not only to your own interests, but also to the interests of others. Your attitude should be the same as that of Christ Jesus ... (4, 5)

The company of God's people consists of those who desire to share the mind of Christ by behaving as servants towards one another. Being united to Christ means that they share in the life of Christ. In this letter Paul was addressing the fellowship as a whole, exhorting the believers to live together in harmony, humility and self-sacrifice. There can be no unity without humility, which in practical terms means exercising self-restraint and demonstrating concern for the wellbeing of others.

When Paul said *'If you have any encouragement ... if any comfort from his love, if any fellowship, ... if any tenderness and compassion'* (1), he was not questioning their Christian experience but rather affirming it. He is saying 'If, as is indeed the case ... ' or, as we might say, 'Since there is encouragement in Christ'. The evidence he observed gave grounds for encouragement, but Paul urged them to greater things that his joy might be complete (2). The church was made up of people from many different backgrounds and with contrasting personalities. They had to learn to get on together. This was made possible not simply because they were kindred spirits but because they shared in the Holy Spirit who bound them together.

Not that everyone was to think the same, for that would entail programming people's minds. Rather it meant to have the same disposition towards each other. Lively discussion among friends is creative as long as it does not destroy friendship and trust. Our emotional investment in our ideas is kept under control out of concern to protect a greater good. We must never forget that the self-sacrificial love of Christ remains our supreme example. Unity is destroyed when each person is out to get his or her own way, or is promoting a hidden agenda. An individual's progress is not like climbing a ladder and knocking people off who are in our way, but rather like a mountaineering team scaling a rock face who are roped together for their mutual help and safety.

Humility (3) is a word often employed to describe the mentality of a slave. In the Roman world it was generally understood to convey the idea of being base, unfit, shabby, mean and of no account – not qualities that anyone wanted to emulate. However, in the Bible it carries a different meaning, referring to people who are lowly and unimportant in their own eyes. It is precisely those persons whom God calls as his servants. Karl Barth, a famous German theologian, comments that the problems of disunity end 'when we discover respect for each other, not on this ground or that, perhaps *without* any grounds, *counter* to any grounds, simply because we are bidden'. We all have a lot to be humble about, and especially as we stand together as forgiven sinners before a holy God.

Having exhorted the Christians in Philippi to be *'of the same mind'*, Paul then identified *whose* mind they were to represent. *'Your attitude should be the same as that of Christ Jesus ... '* (5). We, too, are called upon to reveal the mind of Christ in the way we react and the impression we create. Paul elsewhere described believers as *'the aroma of Christ'* (2 Cor. 2:14, 15). Wherever we go we should leave the fragrance of his presence. So we must ask ourselves, 'Does my life make it easier or harder for people to believe in the existence of a loving, life-transforming God?' Jim Eliot an American missionary who gave his life trying to reach the Auca Indians of Ecuador, prayed, 'Make my life an advertisement to the value of knowing God'. As we contemplate Christ's example of humility and unselfishness our petty quarrelling is shamed into silence.

In what ways do you have to change your thinking and attitude in order to have 'the mind of Christ'?

In verses 6–11 we find preserved a very early hymn of the Christian Church. It is one that exalts Christ as God and then describes his self-emptying to become God's servant here on earth. His life entailed walking a downward path of obedience to the point of dying by crucifixion, which was an agonizing and shameful punishment meted out to criminals. But this tragic event was followed by his resurrection from the dead and his exaltation to heaven, signifying his heavenly Father's vindication of his mission. It is a story of humiliation leading to exaltation.

As we consider the life of Christ we must first consider what he gave up. *'Who, being in very nature God, did not consider equality with God something to be grasped'* (6). He was prepared to exchange heaven's spotless splendour for earth's sinful squalor. Jesus was obedient to his heavenly Father. This is a powerful challenge to those who live in self-centred, possessive societies in which the TV commercials persuade us that 'we owe it to ourselves' to possess this or that status symbol.

The way of the servant is precisely the opposite. It entails pouring out our lives. Jesus *'made himself nothing, taking the very nature of a servant, being made in human likeness'* (7). All that he had he gave in order to enrich others. The account of his life recorded in each of the four Gospels depicts someone who put himself totally at the disposal of people to bring them healing, deliverance, comfort and hope. By *'taking the very nature of a servant'* (7) Jesus forfeited his own rights and privileges in order to give himself completely to those he had come to save.

Second, consider how far he was prepared to go. *'And being found in appearance as a man, he humbled himself and became obedient to death – even death on a cross!'* (8) Humility is not underestimating oneself, but forgetting oneself and acting in disregard for position and reputation. The root of 'humility' is *'humus'*, which means becoming immersed in dirt and decay. Jesus emptied himself in the manner expressed centuries before by the prophet Isaiah, *'... he poured out his life unto death, and was numbered with the transgressors'* (Isa. 53:12). Death by crucifixion was the ultimate in degradation. Any discomfort or discrimination we may experience pales into insignificance in comparison with his sacrifice.

Third, consider what he achieved. The cross that was intended to destroy and permanently silence him became the means by which God achieved his grand purpose for humankind (9). At this point in the hymn it is God the Father who acts on behalf of Christ. As the obedient servant he bore the sins of the world as he suffered on the cross. The Immortal One dies, and is raised by the power of the Holy Spirit. That is the way of the servant, from humiliation to exaltation.

The raising and exaltation of Christ was the most dramatic and extensive swoop in history. And now, as the victorious Christ, he is given the name that is above every name. In ancient thought a *'name'* was a means of describing the inner being, the true nature of that individual. A Nigerian church leader, who was pursuing doctoral studies in the USA, returned to his village during the course of his studies. Meeting with the leaders of his village, one of the tribal elders asked him, 'What is your name?' By this they meant, 'Who have you become during your time away from us?' He wisely replied to the elder, 'I have no name. You must give me my name.'

The Lord is sovereign over the entire universe, '... *that at the name of Jesus every knee should bow, in heaven and on earth and under the earth'* (10). The one who was completely obedient must now be completely obeyed. He speaks not as some despotic ruler but as the one who was himself the servant. Obedience leads to confession *'that Jesus Christ is Lord, to the glory of God the Father'* (11). The affirmation *'Jesus Christ is Lord'* was the earliest confessional formula of the church.

In this hymn we find theology expressed from the heart and earthed in the experience of the Church. Good theology responds to the 'So what?' question. It makes a profound impact on life. In this context it powerfully declares that there is no room for either selfish ambition or superior attitudes in our fellowship and service.

May the mind of Christ my Saviour
Live in me from day to day.
By his love and power controlling
All I do and say.

May the love of Jesus fill me,
As the waters fill the sea.
Him exalting, self abasing
This is victory

The sweet smell of success
Has success ever
smelled so disgusting?

There's a grave whiff
about myrrh, of course,
the perfume of choice
for the God who has everything.

But mix with congealed
blood, sweat and tears
and add the stench of shanties
and tenements and boozers
and mental institutions and
old people's homes and hospitals
and you'll be
stinking
to high heaven.

It could well make you sick;
but the sick could be well.

Relational leadership

1 Thessalonians 2:1-12

... we were delighted to share with you not only the gospel of God but our own lives as well ... (8)

In the New Testament, leadership is never aloof or disconnected from the people who make up the local church. Paul's style of apostolic leadership is highly relational, as is evident from this letter to the Thessalonians. If this was significant for the culture of the first century it is equally appropriate today, especially among younger people, for whom relationships have such a high value. The personal life of the relational leader is an open book. Paul knows that he is under constant scrutiny, not only from his enemies, but also from the new believers who were concerned to know that they were following someone they could trust.

Paul's motives had to be pure and self-evident. He writes to them, *'For the appeal we make to you does not spring from error or impure motives, nor are we trying to trick you'* (3). Furthermore, he recognized that his life was subject to God's scrutiny and nothing escaped his notice. God not only weighs our actions, he tests our hearts, to ensure that we are not simply seeking human approval.

Approval ratings are as likely to go down as suddenly and unpredictably as they go up. Leaders who manoeuvre in accordance with their ratings are likely to be the victims of corresponding mood swings and will end up drifting with the tide, or torn this way and that by conflicting currents.

Could your leadership style be improved?

Leaders can either be a burden or a blessing, depending on whether they simply make demands based on their personal agendas, or whether they are truly serving the needs of the people for whom they are accountable before God. In this portion of Paul's letter, he describes his relationship with the Thessalonians employing three family images: he was among them as a brother, as a nursing mother, and as a father. Each of these images we will now examine in order to appreciate their distinctive contribution to our understanding of leadership. In so doing we will face the challenge of examining our own relationship with fellow believers.

In the first place he described the new believers in Thessalonica as *brothers* (1). Although he is an apostle, he does not stand on his dignity or 'pull rank'. Rather he sets himself on an equal footing with the youngest Christian. We are brothers belonging to the same family, which means that we must not behave as though we were are an only child, with only ourselves to consider. We have to learn to get on with other people. The relationship between brothers and sisters is a robust one. They have to work through their differences, and to learn consideration and cooperation. Brothers and sisters in a family demonstrate different personalities and attitudes influenced by their position in the family, from oldest to youngest child. They have to learn to pull together.

The second image that Paul employs is that of a *mother* (7) caring for her children. The picture that comes to mind is one of devotion, gentleness and dedication. People unaccustomed to infants are awkward and uncomfortable when left 'holding the baby'. Paul knew that new believers needed a great deal of nurture to help them grow in the Christian life. It takes time for them to develop spiritual disciplines and to straighten out their lives. Paul and his team of helpers made sure that they were not rough or off-handed in their handling of new believers. Each person was treated as special, needing personal attention and loving care.

A mother's love is characterized by sacrificial giving of oneself. So Paul reminds the new believers at Thessalonica, *'We loved you so much that we were delighted to share with you not only the gospel of God but our lives as well, because you had become so dear to us'* (8). Consider how family routines revolve around the newborn baby. As the baby grows to become a toddler, it has to be patiently taught by showing and explaining how to develop life skills. Bringing up a child is draining emotionally and spiritually, requiring an inexhaustible supply of patience and forbearance. When we are tempted to pass hasty judgments about the inconsistencies in the life of a younger Christian, we need to remember just how patient God has been with us, not to mention other believers who have had to put up with us.

Lastly, Paul likens himself to a *father* (11), who dealt with them not as though they were someone else's kids, but his own. Dad's role is concerned both with the encouragement and discipline of his children, so that they can eventually stand on their own feet and cope with the world around them. The believers in Thessalonica almost from the first day of their lives as Christians had to face a suspicious and hostile world. They needed to learn to do this with grace and confidence. Paul describes his fatherly role towards them, *'encouraging, comforting and urging you to live lives worthy of God, who calls you into his kingdom and glory'* (12). Now that they had been adopted into God's family, and were representatives of Christ in the world, they had to live up to a high standard. The reputation of the family depended on it!

Keep it in the family

You can't choose your family;
you're stuck with them.
But even though you may
feel like throttling your brother
and cursing your mother
and dissing your father,
isn't it funny how you
won't ever hear a word
said against them?

Blood is thicker than water,
they say. So I eat this bread and
drink this wine,
and I really can't tell you how glad
I am to be thought of as
your own flesh and blood.

day 38 | Wholehearted service

Romans 1:1-17

God, whom I serve with my whole heart in preaching the gospel
of his Son, is my witness how constantly I remember you in my
prayers at all times (9, 10)

At the beginning of Paul's letter to the believers in Rome, Paul
describes himself as a 'servant' – the word actually used is 'slave'.
They represented the majority of the population, and for most of
them there was little hope of gaining their freedom. However, Paul
became one voluntarily. In contrast to the Roman view, the Hebrews
regarded a 'slave of God' as an honourable title.

In our contemporary culture unreserved commitment to anyone
or anything is rarely seen. However, Paul, who served Jesus willingly
and with unqualified allegiance, presents a great challenge to us. The
followers of Christ are described as people who are obedient to the
Gospel (5). They worship Jesus as Lord as well as Saviour.

The order 'slave' and then 'apostle' is significant. The first role was
the necessary prerequisite for the subsequent appointment. In the
Gospels, the followers whom Jesus called to be with him were first
'disciples' (learners or apprentices) before they were sent out as
'apostles'.

The title 'apostle' carries two meanings in the New Testament.
First, it refers to the Twelve Disciples whom Jesus called to be with
him during his earthly ministry. Second, it refers to a wider group of
people, called and commissioned by Jesus to take the Good News into
all the world (see *Day Twenty-Two*). Just as Paul was a servant who
was called to be an apostle, so servant communities are called to be
part of an apostolic church. That means a church that is faithful to
the message delivered by the apostles, as well as being faithful in
continuing that same mission to each succeeding generation.

What is the message that drives Paul's mission? The Good News of
Jesus Christ is no novel message, but one that is well authenticated –
it was promised long ago by the prophets as recorded in the Jewish

Scriptures. The heart of the message was not a philosophy, still less a theory, but a Person. Jesus, the Son of God, not only came to this earth to proclaim the Good News that the Kingdom of God was at hand, he himself was the message. The Kingdom was fully present in his person, and would be provisionally present in the community of those who followed him. Although Jesus came into this world as a helpless baby, he departed this world with a demonstration of resurrection power by the Holy Spirit.

Such was the message that Paul was called to proclaim, and it is that same message that the Church has continued to make known down through the centuries. Paul was no self-appointed apostle, but was called to that task by the Ascended Lord who met with him on the Road to Damascus (Acts 9). That encounter was personally transforming, turning him from a persecutor of Christians and an enemy of Christ to a powerful proclaimer of the Good News. He gratefully acknowledged that his appointment was entirely due to the grace of God (5) and not to any personal merit. Similarly, the servant church is divinely called and commissioned to continue the Great Commission by going into all the world to make disciples among all peoples. That commission has never been rescinded and will remain the marching orders of the Church until the Lord returns.

Paul described the believers in Rome as *'loved by God and called to be saints'* (7). Since *'God so loved the world that he gave his one and only Son'* (John 3:16), he continues to love the world by sending his adopted sons and daughters impassioned to serve and witness in his name. We are all *'saints'* (7) just as we are all 'servants'. 'Saint' signifies those whom God has separated, calling us out of the world to be with him, just as Jesus called out the disciples. But separation

How can you serve God at this time?

does not imply isolation. We are separated *for* rather than separated *from*. We are people set apart for God in order to be sent out into the world.

This calling is imperative for every servant community, but was especially so for the believers in Rome, the epicentre of the Empire.

Not only did all roads lead to Rome, but also all roads led out from Rome. They were not only channels for commerce and conquest but for communication. Along them, news of the faith of the followers of Christ travelled to the far corners of the Roman Empire.

And they were not alone in their outreach. In an earlier letter addressed to the believers in Thessalonica in the province of Achaia (modern southern Greece) Paul had rejoiced that *'The Lord's message rang out from you not only in Macedonia and Achaia – your faith in God has become known everywhere'* (1 Thess. 1:8). As such they had become a model to all the believers in the province.

Paul wanted the believers in Rome to understand that it was because he served God with his *'whole heart'* (9) that he is so committed to preaching the gospel of God's Son. This driving passion is in contrast to many churches today where gospel sharing has become an occasional special effort – a hiccup instead of a heartbeat. Paul's ongoing prayer demonstrates Paul's servant spirit on their behalf. He calls upon God as his witness, *'how constantly I remember you in my prayers at all times'* (9, 10). Prayer permeated his entire life and ministry. It both reflected his concern as well as fuelling his unswerving commitment to the spread of the gospel.

As we know from a number of places in the New Testament, it is the Holy Spirit who bestows all the necessary gifts. They are distributed among the entire membership of the church so that each person can exercise his or her particular ministry. All of ministry is mutual rather than one way so servants must be as willing to receive as they are eager to give. Demonstrating genuine humility and openness of spirit, Paul adds, *'... that you and I may be mutually encouraged by each other's faith'* (12). Every believer has something to give to others in the community, because each has proved the grace of God in human experience. The faith of each person is strengthened as we share with one another how God has helped us through times of perplexity, sickness, fear and apprehension, or supplies our material needs in miraculous ways. As servants we freely share our experiences to meet the needs of others and bring encouragement to them. This is an important part of the spiritual harvest that Paul longed to have among them, consisting not only in the planting of gospel seeds but in bringing those who were already believers to greater spiritual growth and maturity.

The servant community works both intensively and extensively. The apostolic drive is to go both deep and wide. So Paul expressed his profound sense of obligation not only to his own people but to other cultures as well – to educated and uneducated alike. Although he was strategic in his thinking there was nothing elitist in Paul's methods. Whatever the location, or the company, he kept the gospel front and centre. Paul could work equally well in the off-the-beaten-track towns of Galatia as well as in the Imperial capital. No matter how hostile or high ranking his audience he still had full confidence in the gospel: *'I am not ashamed . . . '* (16). May our confidence in that message be equally as strong and may we proclaim it with appropriate boldness through the power of the Holy Spirit.

Body language

Sometimes words aren't enough
to say quite what you mean.
The finest sentences
can make no sense if they don't add up.

In the beginning was the Word,
and the Word became flesh
and spoke of God through what
he did and who he loved.

He taught us how to speak
with more than words;
he gave himself to us
so that we could give ourselves.

We learned to talk in
brand new ways;
perhaps they should call it
body language.

day 39 | Servants not celebrities

1 Corinthians 3:1 – 4:5

What, after all, is Apollos? And what is Paul? Only servants, through whom you came to believe – as the Lord has assigned to each his task (3:5)

We grow in the Christian life not by being preoccupied with ourselves but by serving others. Some Christians do not want to grow, serve and accept responsibility in the Christian life; they simply want to repeat the thrill of their initial experience. They want to be born again, and again, and again! When infants fail to develop, their situation becomes increasingly serious.

Paul was frustrated with the slow progress of the Christians in Corinth. They still needed nursing when they should have been able to feed themselves. They were still on a basic milk diet when they should have been able to cope with solid food. Clear evidence of their lack of maturity was provided by their constant bickering prompted by jealousy and cliquishness. Paul had already referred to this sad state of affairs in the opening section of his letter. Immediately following his greeting, in which he affirms them for eloquence and knowledge and the abundance of spiritual gifts that was evident in the fellowship, he makes his appeal to deal with the divisions in their community.

The problem was that they had turned the servants, whom God had sent to establish the church in Corinth, into celebrities. The church had become divided into groups who were at loggerheads with each other, as they rallied around a respected name, such as Paul, Apollos, Cephas (Peter) and Jesus himself. Each identified with a well-known name in order to give their group status. Perhaps those who identified with Jesus were thinking 'Cap that!' as they looked down on the others.

One group cannot claim Christ for itself in competition with another. No group has exclusive access to a heavenly 'hotline'. It was Christ, not Paul, who was crucified that we might be reconciled to

God. And it is in Christ's name, not Paul's, that we are baptized. In almost every case Paul refused to baptize converts himself in order to avoid the possibility of people then claiming to be special.

Servants who are in the public eye may find themselves having to resist firmly every attempt to make them the focus of undue attention. Paul emphasized, as he did on so many occasions, that although an apostle, he was first and foremost a servant. He was simply the channel through whom God worked in order that they might have the opportunity to hear and respond to the Good News of Christ.

Do you have a spiritual hero who has come between you and Christ?

It is significant that he asked not '*Who* is Apollos? And *who* is Paul?' but '*What* is Apollos? And *what* is Paul?'. By this expression he focused the attention of the Corinthians on the different *functions* that each of the people named fulfilled rather than on their personalities. They were '*Only servants, through whom you came to believe*' (5) and were simply doing their God-assigned task.

God's servants in every age must take equal care to avoid gathering a following, especially at the expense of another group. So much church growth consists of transfer growth rather than new growth. Servants who are ego driven simply want to attract a following without enquiring too closely as to where the people they are attracting are coming from.

One servant should not be set against another, or one compared unfavourably with another. We all suffer when our weaknesses and limitations are compared with the strengths of someone else. Such comparisons are inappropriate, for we each have our own distinctive contribution to make. This was the case with Paul and Apollos, who had different personalities and gifts, with each doing the job that the Lord had assigned.

Paul described himself as a planter of the seed of the Gospel (6). As an apostle he was a pioneer in spreading the word of God, in leading people to faith in Christ as Saviour and Lord, and in forming new communities of believers. As soon as a work was established in a city or region he would then move on to new areas of work, periodically retracing his steps to give further encouragement and guidance to the new churches.

Apollos' task was different. He was the cultivator of the seed that Paul had planted (6). Apollos was a Jew from the city of Alexandria in North Africa. We first hear of him in the city of Ephesus, where Aquila and Priscilla befriended him and helped him to a fuller understanding of the gospel (see *Day 35*). He was described as a knowledgeable person with a profound knowledge of the Scriptures and as an enthusiastic and eloquent speaker. From Ephesus, Apollos travelled to Corinth where he distinguished himself as an apologist in debate with the Jews. His continuing presence in Corinth evidently resulted in his attracting a personal following.

In describing their functions, Paul placed emphasis on the role God plays in the communication of the Gospel. Only God could bring about the miracle of germination, without which all their planting and cultivating would have been completely futile (7). As servants they must work together in proper sequence and in full dependence on God. Servants do not work in isolation, but as members of a team. But more than that, the way in which they relate to one another is a demonstration of the power of the Gospel, which is a message of reconciliation. A church or fellowship torn apart by internal strife is not a credible communicator.

Paul then changed the imagery from plant cultivation to building construction (10). His task as an apostle was to lay a firm foundation on the bed-rock of Jesus Christ. There was no other place to build. Foundations are below the surface and are neither attractive nor spectacular. But as Jesus pointed out, when we build in the wrong place, with inadequate foundations, then the building will topple as soon as it is buffeted by storms and inundated by floods (Matt. 7:24–27). It is only the house built on the rock that will survive. That foundation consists not only of hearing but obeying the words of Jesus. Servants who are called to spread the gospel and establish new groups of believers need to be equally careful as they lay spiritual foundations.

People like Apollos, who build upon the foundations laid by others, need to be no less careful. Upon the firm foundation a substantial structure needs to be skilfully constructed. Following Paul's analogy, we must build with fire-resistant materials. If we use shoddy materials and allow slap-dash workmanship then we will be held accountable (12, 13). For in kingdom building we are called to build to last. Severe trials lie ahead that will reveal the quality of our workmanship. If nothing survives of our work, due to penny-pinching, corner-cutting and carelessness, then we will suffer loss. We will have nothing to show for our labours. But although our service will be judged our salvation will not be denied.

Although servants are there to serve, and not to attract attention to themselves, they are still individuals of intrinsic worth. They are not mere replaceable and dispensable cogs in a machine. Collectively we are the body of Christ. Paul also described the Corinthians as *'God's temple'* (3:16). They were not a heap of bricks, but living stones, built into a beautiful structure that gives glory to God. Their community life announced to the world that God was to be encountered in their midst. Everybody is valued, so there is zero toleration for prideful boasting. Our scale of values is different from the criteria that the world applies.

Servants neither disempower nor exclude others. Eugene Peterson in *The Message* paraphrases Paul's description of his role and that of Apollos' as *'guides into God's most sublime secrets, not security guards posted to protect them'*. Every servant is accountable to his or her master. What counts is the Lord's evaluation of each of his servants, which means that we can ride the unfair criticism that others may level at us. Paul reminded himself, the Corinthians and us, that the Lord is the judge before whom we will all one day have to give an account. On that day he will not only weigh our actions but also expose our motives. There will be no pedestals for celebrities in heaven. As servants the highest accolade we can receive is to hear him say, 'Well done, good and faithful servant!'

Consider the following
I follow Paul
I follow Cephas
I wake up with Benny Hinn.

Perhaps it's time
I made a name
for myself.

It must be easy
to be a big fish
in a small pond.

Jesus Christ,
Superstar,
You're quite a hit.

What must I do to
follow in your famous
footsteps?

Finishing well

2 Timothy 3:10 – 4:8

I have fought the good fight, I have finished the race, I have kept the faith (4:7). But as for you, continue in what you have learned and have become convinced of, because you know those from whom you have learned it ... (3:14)

Our reflections on some of the great leaders of God's people provide both an inspiration and a warning. On the one hand we have seen the great heights to which people of humble origins rose. Yet on the other hand we have seen how vulnerable they were on occasion, and how some, like King Saul, became tragic figures towards the end of their lives. Our concern in this last study is on how we can finish well. Paul provides an inspiring example as one who not only finished well, but in so doing also left a legacy that continues to this day.

Here Paul provides both an example and an exhortation. His life was an open book that Timothy had examined with great care. Timothy knew that the apostle Paul, who had served as his mentor and coach for a number of years, was a person he could trust and emulate. He knew his heart and the message that inspired Paul's life. Timothy had seen Paul's unswerving commitment to the commission that the Lord had entrusted to him, to take the good news to the Gentiles. Timothy had observed that Paul's whole way of life rang true with the standards he set for other believers. Timothy knew from personal experience Paul's unshakeable confidence in God

What legacy are you leaving behind? One that will last?

and his resilience and perseverance in the face of adversity, which would have crushed a lesser man. Paul had made it clear that other believers must be prepared to receive similar treatment (3:12; see also 2 Cor. 12:9–10 and 1 Thess. 3:4).

It is not only the example of Paul that sustained Timothy over the years, but also the teaching he received from infancy from his mother Eunice and his grandmother Lois. These godly individuals had taught him the Old Testament scriptures, causing him to value them as the inspired word of God and helping him to apply them to his life as a follower of Jesus. No doubt Timothy was also encouraged by the witness of the other new believers in Lystra and Iconium, where he was held in such high regard. Under the training of Paul he had been equipped as a pastor, teacher and evangelist. He had been given a clear grasp of the gospel so that he could confront the heretics and their teaching that was prevalent in Ephesus. The Scriptures also provided the authority he needed to correct those whose lives did not conform to their Christian profession. And Timothy himself needed to ensure that he was a man of God *'thoroughly equipped for every good work'* (3:17). Just as an athlete in training for the games had to be at the peak of physical fitness, so he had to be spiritually fit to stay the course and provide an example and encouragement to others.

Paul gives Timothy a clear charge to continue to proclaim the word of God. While we are not all called to be public speakers we are commissioned to bear a faithful witness in our personal conversation. Like Timothy we are to be alert to take advantage of every opportunity, whether or not we feel up to it at the time. Timothy is ordered to correct those who are heading in wrong directions, to rebuke those who will not heed the voice of their conscience or the warnings of friends, as well as to encourage the fainthearted. Paul knows that Timothy is both youthful and timid, so needs these reminders not to shirk his responsibilities. He is to be diligent to discharge all the duties of his ministry (4:5) as a teacher and evangelist.

While Timothy still has a great distance to cover in the race of life, Paul is nearing its end. He writes from a Roman prison, knowing that his days are numbered, *'I have fought the good fight, I have finished the race, I have kept the faith'* (4:7). He now awaits the victor's crown. He has passed on the baton to Timothy. Although he is approaching the finishing line, it is but the end of his lap; the relay continues to this day and until the Lord returns.

Who is passing the baton to us? And to whom will we in turn pass it on when our lap is ended? The victor's reward is not confined to the all-time greats, such as Paul, but is awarded to the entire team – to all who await the Lord's appearing with eager anticipation (4:8).

Passing on

What I have learned,
I will now pass on.
What I have seen,
I will now pass on.
What I have experienced,
I will now pass on.
What I have heard,
I will now pass on.
What I have received,
I will now pass on.
What I have noticed,
I will now pass on.
What I have gathered,
I will now pass on.

One day, I know, I will pass on myself;
Until then, I will gladly give my all.